THE DISCIPLINE OF TEAMS

A Mindbook-Workbook for Delivering Small Group Performance

JON R. KATZENBACH
DOUGLAS K. SMITH

John Wiley & Sons, Inc.

New York • Chichester • Weinheim • Brisbane • Singapore • Toronto

Published by John Wiley & Sons, Inc.

Published simultaneously in Canada.

This publication is designed to provide accurate and authoritative information in regard to the subject matter covered. It is sold with the understanding that the publisher is not engaged in rendering professional services. If professional advice or other expert assistance is required, the services of a competent professional person should be sought.

Library of Congress Cataloging-in-Publication Data:

Katzenbach, Jon R., 1932–
    The discipline of teams : a mindbook-workbook for delivering small group performance / Jon Katzenbach, Doug Smith.
      p. cm.
    Includes bibliographical references and index.
    ISBN 0-471-38254-X (cloth : alk. paper)
      1. Teams in the workplace.   I. Smith, Douglas K., 1949–   II. Title.
    HD66 .K382 2001
    654.4'036—dc21

                                                   00-054565

Printed in the United States of America.

10 9 8 7 6 5 4 3 2

CONTENTS

ACKNOWLEDGMENTS

This book owes its origins to *The Wisdom of Teams,* and the research and consulting efforts that are reflected therein. We would be remiss in not acknowledging those who contributed to that effort, even though it dates back to 1993. In addition, both of us want to acknowledge how much we have learned during the intervening years from people and teams who have worked to apply the principles, conclusions and ideas from *Wisdom* in the real world of teaming. We have heard from literally hundreds of readers whose comments, questions and experiences led us to write *Discipline.* Unfortunately, though not surprisingly, there have been far too many of these "contributing practitioners" to mention individually.

We also benefited from some recent research efforts with respect to virtual teaming. Several members of the professional staff of Katzenbach Partners LLC volunteered their professional and personal time and experiences to probe specific virtual teaming situations for us, and we want to thank them individually: Susie Banakarim, Amrita Bhandari, Courtney Cannon, Amy Gallo, Brigitte Lippmann, Stacy Palestrant, Giridhar Srinivasan, and Roopa Unnikrishnan. We appreciate the support of Marc Feigen, Niko Canner, and Amy McDonald in making the time of these consultants available. Most importantly we, once again, thank Debbie Shortnacy for her diligent support throughout the research and the writing.

We also want to thank Richard Cavanagh and his staff at The Conference Board for helping us identify several companies who gave us access to virtual team situations. Those deserving special mention include Jackie Moore of American Express and Martin Finegan of KPMG. In addition, we are particularly grateful to Hervé Martin and Nadia Circelli of STMicroelectronics, as well as Fabrice Guerrier of ST University for their dedication and hard work in helping us observe a particularly complex global team effort.

Last but not least, we once again acknowledge the patience and forbearance of our wives and children, since much of the work was done on nights and weekends normally reserved for family time.

Discipline Is Wisdom

The most important characteristic of teams is discipline; not bonding, togetherness, or empowerment. Perhaps the finest examples of small group of performance are in the U.S. Marine Corps (USMC). Some of the small groups qualify as teams and some do not. But whatever small group configuration is required, the USMC invariably uses the right one at the right time. The reason is discipline. Discipline is a three-dimensional concept for the USMC. Top-down command and control is alive and well, but it is no match for the peer discipline and self-discipline that create value-driven marines. (Figure 1 illustrates the true dimensions of performance discipline.)

It is this three-dimensional discipline that ensures that the leadership role in a USMC fire team will shift, depending on who has the high ground. This same discipline motivates rifle platoon leadership teams, where a gunnery sergeant might tell his captain to change the intended tactical maneuver because he, the gunny, perceives a better way. It is this discipline that motivates every rifleman to act on the intent of leaders two levels up, since intent always takes precedence over any direct command to the contrary. Moreover, the USMC can

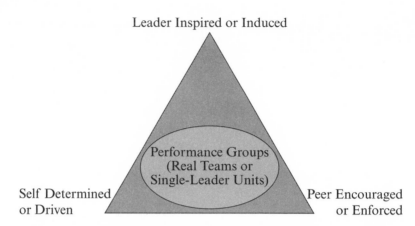

FIGURE 1 The three dimensions of performance discipline

apply real-team discipline with the same conviction and facility as they apply the single-leader discipline, for which they are better known. Marines are masters of team performance because they are proficient at not one, but two disciplines that create versatile, powerful performance units.

It is not happenstance that this book is entitled *The Discipline of Teams,* the sequel and companion to our earlier work, *The Wisdom of Teams.* In fact, for the first book, we might have easily chosen *discipline* for the title instead of *wisdom,* since we certainly recognized its importance at the time. We even called our definition of teams a *discipline.* What we failed to appreciate fully, however, is the difficulty many would encounter in differentiating and integrating the team and single-leader disciplines. That difficulty, more than anything else, warrants this sequel, which we sincerely hope will provide additional help to the readers of and believers in *The Wisdom of Teams* as they work hard to get real teams in the right places at the right times for the right reasons.

Nearly a decade has passed since our initial work on *The Wisdom of Teams.* Since its initial publication in 1993, the book has been translated into over fifteen languages and serves as a standard text in the curriculum of several leading universities, indicating that the book has stood the test of time. Over the years, we have continued to work with and learn about small groups (from all sectors of the economy and all parts of the globe) whose performance increasingly distinguishes those organizations that succeed from those that don't.

In his review of *The Wisdom of Teams,* John Byrne of *Business Week* called teams "the essential building block of the organization of the future." Clearly, that organization of the future is the organization of today. And, unlike a decade ago, few argue with the critical role and contribution of teams. The concept of teaming was still relatively fresh, if not controversial, in the late 1980s. When mentioned in top management circles, teaming elicited cynical smirks just as often as enthusiastic smiles. In fact, one of our purposes in writing *The Wisdom of Teams* was to help line managers and executives make better use of teams as performance units rather than as human resource ploys to promote involvement and empowerment. The situation is markedly different today. Teams and teaming are as much a fixture in good management practice as planning, budgeting, personnel performance reviews, strategy, information technology, and other elements of organizational design. We find it hard to imagine a thriving, successful enterprise with no experience or use of teams.

So, why a sequel? For two reasons: First, we believe we have gained significant experience and insight about what groups can do to ensure they apply the right discipline at the right time; second, the world of teams has evolved over the past ten years in ways that increase both the importance of and challenges to achieving team performance. Virtual teaming is perhaps the single, most indicative development in that regard. Groups all over the world now can utilize countless new technological tools for working together more effectively. These tools permit people to interact across far greater geographic, cultural, language, and time-zone barriers than ever before. At the same time, new *groupware,* both hardware and software, complicates, confuses, and subverts efforts to apply the team discipline. We believe these challenges are worthy of thoughtful exploration and commentary.

Despite the rapid spread of teaming for performance purposes, we have little trouble identifying organizations and people who flounder in their use of teams. Understanding the value and potential of teams has proved to be much easier than applying the discipline required in achieving team performance. As a result, far too many people still think of *team* as a name for an organizational unit or a set of companionable feelings. Yet, as we suggested in *The Wisdom of Teams* and will further explore and provide guidance for in this book, teaming works best when treated as a discipline for small group performance. Moreover, teaming is only one of the two essential disciplines for achieving small group performance. The other is the *single-leader discipline,* a clarifying label change from *The Wisdom of Teams* where we called it *working-group discipline.* With the single-leader discipline, a formal leader is in control and responsible for the direction and success of the group. This is not so with the team discipline. When small groups apply the team discipline appropriately, only the team can succeed, and only the team can fail. Of course individual accountability still matters, but unless it is combined with mutual accountability and common levels of commitment to achieve collective results, teams cannot perform.

Disciplines are not checklists of best practices, but according to *Webster's Collegiate Dictionary,* they do imply "orderly or prescribed conduct and patterns of behavior." More important, disciplines are grounded in fundamental principles, and those who would benefit from applying those disciplines must continually adhere to the underlying principles. For example, there is a discipline for practicing yoga, piano, and golf. There is even a discipline for losing weight. Consequently, if you wish to lose weight, you must eat less, eat more wisely, and exercise more. If you do each of those three things only once and check them off your list, you will not lose weight. Only through repeated and persistent application of all three can you expect to meet significant weight loss goals.

So, too, with both the team and single-leader disciplines for small group performance. Certainly, it is critical to distinguish one from the other. It is also important to recognize how these disciplined performance units differ from the more common effective groups that are so often labeled *teams,* but produce little more than congenial interaction and effective group dynamics. In Chapter 1, we will review the principles and behavior patterns for each of the *performance disciplines.* In Chapter 2, we explore the impact of *virtual teaming.* In Chapter 3, we suggest how your small group can use specific performance challenges to choose when to use one versus the other. If you apply these disciplines consistently, your group can expect to advance well beyond that of an effective group in terms of performance results. Conversely, if you use either discipline sporadically or merely as a checklist, your performance will fall short. The key point, however, is that these are time-tested disciplines that result in higher levels of small group performance. They are not names for types of groups; nor are they labels for feelings of togetherness or individual versus group identity.

Every small group we have ever been part of or privy to has had to figure out how to get along and communicate with one another well enough to deliver performance. Getting along, that is, effective group dynamics, is certainly important. But getting along is as critical to the single-leader discipline as it is to the team discipline. Far too many people, including experts, speak, act, manage, lead, and advise as though getting along, or improving group dynamics, is the same thing as teaming. It is not.

By contrast, when small groups emphasize performance as their touchstone, they not only achieve significant performance results, but they also learn to respect and like each other. We are not arguing against the value of bonding, trust, and mutual respect for small groups. In fact, one of our fundamental beliefs is that *a common performance objective is much more motivating for effective teams than the desire to be a team.* The same applies to the single-leader discipline: *performance objectives linked to individual accountability motivate small group performance much more than the desire for individual opportunity and distinction.* Small groups that emphasize performance will differentiate goals that warrant the single-leader approach from those that warrant the team approach. As a result, the members of the small group are much more likely to build and sustain trust-based working relationships than groups who obsess on relationships, feelings, and roles.

Of course, to use performance effectively as a guide in choosing between and applying the two disciplines, your group must be clear about performance. Your group must first decide that you want and need to be more than an effective group. Does performance matter or not? Following the publication of *The Wisdom of Teams*, perhaps nothing surprised us more than the difficulties people in organizations have in articulating specific performance goals. With the sometime exception of financial goals, people in most organizations chase after activity-based goals, or goals that describe the activities to be done, instead of the performance impacts or outcomes those activities are supposed to produce. Chapter 3 introduces you to the critical distinction between *outcome-based goals* and *activity-based goals*. Chapter 4 discusses how your small group can create and manage itself according to a *performance agenda* that specifies the outcomes and helps you match those outcomes with disciplines and resources.

If your group carefully distinguishes goals best approached through teaming from those best accomplished through the single-leader discipline, you will greatly increase your performance potential. Moreover, when your group chooses the team discipline, your attention to performance will guide you in applying the six basic principles of the team discipline as defined in *The Wisdom of Teams:* " . . . a small number of people with complementary skills who are committed to a common purpose, performance goals, and approach for which they hold themselves mutually accountable."

Chapters 5, 6, and 7 offer guidance regarding the application of the principles to your team performance challenges. Chapter 5 reviews what you can do to ensure that your group stays small and that the members have complementary skills. Chapter 6 provides guidance and exercises to enable your team to develop a common purpose, common performance goals, and a commonly agreed-upon working approach. Chapter 7 discusses how you can know whether you have integrated mutual accountability with individual accountability and, if not, what to do about it. Chapter 8 returns to virtual teaming to explore the obstacles and opportunities it creates. Finally, Chapter 9 contains exercises to pinpoint what to do when your team gets stuck, as all teams do. Chapter 9 will also assist you in determining if and when your team should completely reengineer or end the effort.

In supplying detailed guidance, plus dozens of exercises

for small groups, the book is a direct response to countless requests for a companion or sequel workbook to *The Wisdom of Teams*. To that end, this book offers new background, frameworks, tools, and exercises for converting broad purposes into specific, outcome-based performance goals. Moreover, we also illustrate how to use those goals to choose between the team and single-leader disciplines. In so doing, the book drives home a central point that we took for granted in *The Wisdom of Teams*. Understanding the differences between effective groups and disciplined performance units is a lot easier than integrating the two different disciplines to achieve significantly higher performance results.

This book, however, has an important additional purpose: to shed new light on the rapidly expanding world of *virtual teaming*. Specifically, we want to help groups who use information and communications technology to accomplish group work and performance. In the years since publishing *The Wisdom of Teams*, there has been an explosion in virtual teaming and virtual work. People now regularly collaborate through the medium of technology across geographic, organizational, and time-zone boundaries. It is difficult to identify an organization anywhere in the world that is not experiencing this shift. And there have been hundreds of books and articles written to guide people toward more effective use of the technology.

Our purpose here is to discuss the opportunities and effects of the new technology on the challenge of using the two disciplines for small-group performance. In Chapter 2, we stress that while technology can enable the two disciplines, it does not change them or the value of rigorously applying them. Two extreme claims are often made about group work technology. One contends that groupware actually prevents real teams; the other contends that groupware greatly enables team performance. Both oversimplify the likely impact of this rapidly evolving arena. In addition, far too many observers have implied that technology revolutionizes or supplants management disciplines. It does not. The two key management disciplines for small performance units, team and single leader, remain the same, whether your group works in the same room or across many time zones and geographic locations. Nonetheless, both teaming and single-leader efforts are increasingly affected by group work technology. As we discuss in Chapter 8, this technology makes applying the team discipline both easier and harder. And, in our opinion, the underlying character of the technology reinforces a bias within small groups that inadvertently favors, often unwisely, the single-leader discipline. Nonetheless, the value of choosing and rigorously applying the two disciplines remains unchanged.

Chapters 2 and 8 are focused exclusively on how virtual groups can best use technology to achieve performance, as well as several critical pitfalls to avoid. However, throughout the book, we also highlight if and when virtual work and virtual teaming are truly different from nonvirtual efforts.

To summarize, this book has several purposes and objectives. First, there is a growing need to distinguish effective, congenial groups from disciplined performance units. More important, the book distinguishes, clarifies, and assists you in applying the two essential disciplines for small group performance: the team and single-leader. And, it will provide the direction and help small groups need to convert ambiguous, activity-based objectives into specific, outcome-based goals. We explore ways that small groups and their leaders can use performance goals as the basis for choosing and applying the two disciplines. For groups applying the team discipline, each chapter offers detailed advice, tools, and exercises to help ensure success. Most important, perhaps, every exercise in this book can be done by the members of the small groups themselves, without the aid of outside facilitators. Finally, we have tried to distinguish the most critical aspects of technology and virtual teaming so that groups can apply the time-tested disciplines for small group performance across multiple locations and time zones.

Once again, however, we are sure that we address a moving target. By the time you read this book, the organizational and technological context for teams and single-leader units will have evolved. New challenges, new approaches, and new dimensions of teaming continually emerge. Nonetheless, we believe the best way to deal with these subjects continues to be a relentless focus on the performance challenge you face and rigorous application of the appropriate discipline. The wisdom of teams continues to be the discipline of teams.

CHAPTER 1

Mastering Two Disciplines—Not One

It is more than instinct alone . . .

We have all been part of a small group that somehow came together to accomplish unexpected feats as a team. The personal chemistry was right, the circumstances were compelling, and the group jelled. We have all also been part of small-group efforts that fell apart because of a misplaced concern about becoming a team, when, instead, the situation called for one clear leader to take charge. So how can you get team performance when it counts, without losing the power of single leadership and individual accountability when they count? This is a matter of applying the right discipline at the right time against the right challenge.

There are two key disciplines of small-group performance: the team discipline and the single-leader discipline. The *team discipline* promises a great deal of versatility and collective power when deployed against a challenge that warrants and demands a team. Many important performance challenges, however, do not benefit from teaming. For example, a half dozen salespeople, assigned to separate territories, typically will maximize sales results through the sum of their individual efforts. Challenges like this are best achieved through the *single-leader discipline,* which is defined as the sum of separate, individual contributions directed and managed by a single leader. (Please note: In *The Wisdom of Teams,* we called this the "working group" discipline. Over the past decade, we and those we consult with have found "single leader" to be a more useful descriptor.)

Members of small groups must be conscious and deliberate about when, where, and how to use the team discipline versus the single-leader discipline. Not surprisingly, both disciplines are effective if used in the right situations, and a balanced leadership approach will integrate the two, rather than constantly favoring one over the other. Unfortunately, too many leaders neither integrate nor balance these two disciplines. Instead, they instinctively, if not blindly, follow the single-leader approach, as though it were the *only* way to manage. Also, they may put more or less emphasis on teamwork, in the sense of togetherness, depending on the leader's personal style.

Leaders with this unfortunate habit and mind-set, together with the groups they lead, increasingly fail because performance results in today's fast-moving and challenging environment demand mastery of both disciplines. Intentionally or not, such leaders foster what we call *compromise units,* small groups who fail to grasp and apply either of the two disciplines, and become dysfunctional.

People in compromise units do not recognize that team performance requires the team discipline. Instead, members of such groups and their leaders never get beyond inadequate appeals to teamwork. They cry out to "be more of a team" and complain about "not getting along" or being insufficiently "empowered." Leaders of such groups often go hot and cold in their approaches, first commanding members to "Be a team!" then backing off with the hope that a real team will somehow coalesce. They seldom do. Yet, when leaders retreat, and the group fails to apply the discipline of team basics, a confused and leaderless gang inevitably results. Compromise units are the worst of both worlds, allowing performance to deteriorate because the leader and members of the group have neglected to apply the two key disciplines of small-group performance.

Learning how and when to apply the two disciplines for small-group performance begins with recognizing that each discipline supports *the five basic elements of effective group work*. It is important to remember that an effective group is a significant step below a performance unit. Nonetheless, neither of the two small-group performance units, real team or single-leader group, can realize its performance potential unless the five elements are in place. First, the group has or develops *an understandable charter* that provides the group with a reason and purpose for working together; however, the charter is not necessarily focused on performance. Second, the members of the group *communicate and coordinate effectively* to allow constructive interactions involving all of the members. Third, the members of the group establish *clear roles and areas of responsibility,* which allow them to work individually or collectively. Fourth, the members create *a time-efficient process,* minimizing wandering discussions and wasted time. And, finally, the group develops *a sense of accountability* helping each member understand individual contributions to the success of the group; hence, progress can be monitored and evaluated accordingly. Figure 1.1 illustrates how these elements of effective group work provide the base on which performance units develop. The essential difference

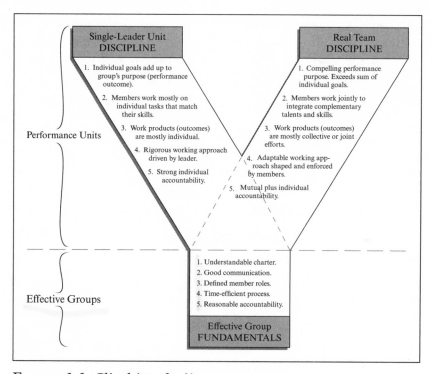

FIGURE 1.1 Climbing the Y
Source: Copyright by Katzenbach Partners LLC.

between an effective group and the two performance units is in the clarity of the group's focus on performance and the rigor with which the members of the group apply the appropriate discipline required by the performance challenge.

The team discipline and the single-leader discipline are two distinctly different managerial approaches. Both are required for an effective group to become a performance unit. Leaders and the other members of small groups must master all three branches of the Y: (1) the elements of effective group work; (2) the discipline of single-leader groups, and (3) the basics of real-team performance. Optimizing the value of small-group work requires understanding each of the branches and knowing how to use performance as a guide for deciding when to branch left (single leader) versus right (team).

The Single-Leader Discipline

The single-leader discipline revolves around one leader. The leader, often in consultation with the group, determines the performance-based reason and purpose for group work, makes the decisions, establishes the required individual contributions and group pattern of communications, and determines the requirements of success and how and when to evaluate progress. In the single-leader discipline, the formal leader:

1. Makes and communicates decisions for the group. The members of the group respect the decisions because the leader has the required formal authority, as well as recognized experience, proven judgment, and relevant knowledge of the performance situation. Indeed, members of the group *expect* the leader to make the decisions. While consultation can be a part of the decision process, the leader makes the final decision.

2. Sets the performance goals and determines individual responsibilities. While the goal-setting process often involves open communication and two-way negotiation, the leader has the final say about what constitutes an appropriate goal for each member, as well as for the group as a whole. Members often provide important input in this process, but the leader establishes the goals.

3. Sets the pace and determines the working approach. The leader monitors the progress and pace of each person's effort and motivates individuals, as well as the group as a whole. The leader determines the overall working approach, which reflects a series of individual contributions based on stable, well-defined, individual roles for each member of the group. The leader acceler-

ates or slows the pace by setting deadlines for the group and its members.

4. Evaluates the results. The leader assesses individual results, as well as overall group progress, and makes adjustments as needed. The leader is responsible for achieving group results that are acceptable to higher-level managers. Throughout the process, the leader recognizes and rewards the contributions and results of individuals.

5. Establishes benchmarks and standards. The leader fosters sharing of ideas among the members and encourages best practices both within and outside the group, ensuring effective group communication between members and outsiders. In most cases, the leader makes the final determination of the best standards for the group.

6. Maintains control of the group effort by clarifying individual accountability and emphasizes consequence management. As a result, the members of the group are clear about their roles, specific goals, expected end-products, manner of interaction with others, and deadlines. The leader determines the measures that apply to individuals and to the group as a whole. In the final analysis, the leader is in control. Furthermore, the members of the group, as well as senior management outside the group, expect the leader to be in control.

The single-leader discipline is a familiar and essential part of all well-managed organizations. Throughout history, most organizational departments and business units have been led primarily in this mode. Team gurus and enthusiasts aside, we believe most leaders and employees are more comfortable working within the single-leader discipline because each team member knows what is expected and how performance will be assessed. Perhaps what is more revealing is that being accountable for your own, individual goals and actions is preferable, clearer, and easier than the shared responsibility that characterizes the team discipline. With every good intention, we may advocate teamwork, but our actions all too often favor the single-leader discipline mind-sets and behaviors.

The Team Discipline

As useful, valuable, and time-honored as the single-leader discipline is to small-group performance, it is not the only way, or always the best way, to manage small groups. The team discipline, which demands shared leadership and mutual accountability is the alternative. When groups effectively apply the team discipline, the group, not the formal leader, determines the performance rationale and purpose for group work, and the group establishes the required individual and collective contributions and pattern of communications. The group also sets the requirements for success and how and when to evaluate progress.

The team discipline requires peer- and self-enforcement and is described in *The Wisdom of Teams* as "a small number of people with complementary skills who are committed to a common purpose, performance goals, and approach for which they hold themselves mutually accountable." These six elements are reviewed thoroughly in Chapter 5 (small number and complementary skills), Chapter 6 (common purpose, goals, and working approach), and Chapter 7 (mutual accountability). Instead of elaborating element by element at this point, the following paragraphs highlight how the team discipline differs from the single-leader discipline.

1. In the team discipline, decisions are made by the appropriate people. Sometimes the decision-maker is, in fact, the designated team leader and sometimes it is the whole group. But, far more often, decisions are made by the person or people whose skills and experience best qualify them to decide. This is why team basics require a set of complementary skills. Groups who apply the team discipline do not require consensus decisions. (For more on the dangers of consensus decision-making, see Chapter 6.) In fact, the group rarely even votes. Instead, decisions get made by those the group believes best positioned to do so, usually as a result of talent, skill, experience, and assigned work task. The leader only intervenes when group members are incapable or unwilling to reach a decision. In contrast to the clear, unvarying, decision-making authority that characterizes the single-leader discipline, leadership and choice making shifts and is shared among the members in groups using the team discipline.

2. Goals of groups using the team discipline are set and affirmed individually and collectively by the group. While the designated leader may argue persuasively for certain goals, the goals are not set until the members of the group have explored the implications, wrestled with the trade-offs, and developed a shared understanding and mutual sense of commitment. This process differs from the characteristic, one-on-one negotiation between each member and the leader in the single-leader discipline. Moreover, in the team discipline the group clearly differentiates between individual goals and collective goals. (In fact, the achievement of collective goals is the joint responsibility of two or more mem-

bers.) When groups are using the team discipline, the number and value of collective goals invariably outweigh the number and value of individual goals.

3. In the team discipline, the pace and working approach are set by the group, making the approach a matter of shared commitment. The team chooses the best way to distribute and integrate work, manage logistics and administration, and establish and enforce norms for each other. More important, the roles and contributions of the members shift to fit different performance-task needs, instead of remaining predictable, stable, and relatively inflexible as in the single-leader approach.

4. In the team discipline, the group rigorously and consistently evaluates its own results. Because the purpose and goals of the team require similar levels of commitment from all of the members, the group assesses its progress *as a team*. The team is its own toughest critic, and members are less forgiving of performance shortfalls than their sponsors or even the leader. Members of a team hold each other accountable to a greater degree than they are held accountable by either the leader or the sponsoring authority. Furthermore, when teams evaluate progress, the dialogue is open, nonhierarchical, and more focused on performance progress and the entire effort of the group than on individual performance.

5. In the team discipline, the members of the group set high standards. These demanding standards arise from the compelling performance purpose to which all members are committed. Because of their shared commitment, the members of the group seek out tough stan-

dards and high comparisons for themselves. The group is seldomly satisfied with the standards or benchmarks used elsewhere in the organization. It is not uncommon for a team to establish a set of goals that exceeds the goals set in its charter from the sponsoring authority. Groups using the team discipline thrive on clearing a bar that others would not attempt.

6. Members of groups using the team discipline hold themselves individually and mutually accountable. With groups applying the team discipline, it is very difficult (if not impossible) for any one member to fail—only the team can succeed or fail. Team members are not easy on one another in this respect. Yet, they are extremely flexible and adaptable in helping each other to contribute to the fullest extent possible and to develop new skill levels in the process. In marked contrast, the single-leader discipline almost exclusively emphasizes individual accountability and development. Indeed, mutual accountability for shared purpose and goals may be *the* hallmark of the team discipline.

Read the preceding two sections on the single-leader discipline and the team discipline again in conjunction with the Y chart in the first section of this chapter. Note how each discipline builds upon and extends the five basics of effective group work: (1) a clearly understood purpose and rationale for group work—though not necessarily performance focused; (2) open communication and coordination among all of the members—though always within a predictable meeting agenda; (3) clear roles and areas of responsibility as to how work will get done—though seldom differentiated by individual versus collective work product needs; (4) a time-efficient process that minimizes "group groping"—though seldom variable by group task; and (5) a sense of who is accountable for what and what success looks like and how to evaluate progress—though seldom rigorously enforced. In short, these fundamentals enable groups to work effectively, but not to perform exceptionally.

Yet, as you reread these two sections, we urge you to learn the distinctions between these two separate performance disciplines for small groups as well as the fundamentals of effective group work. The two disciplines should feel different. For example, if you consider a small group in which you currently participate, you ought to find it easy to use the above descriptions to identify which of these two management disciplines is being used and if your efforts are best characterized as an effective group or worse, a compromise unit.

Table 1.1 provides a model to highlight the key differences between effective groups who merely interact well, and performance units who apply discipline to achieve success.

A balanced approach to small-group effectiveness starts with the conscious choice of which discipline will work best for a particular performance challenge. *Note:* these two disciplines lead to performance unit results—they are not simply the names for two types of work groups. We are not suggesting or encouraging leaders and groups to choose between being a team or being a single-leader group. In fact, we strongly warn against that mindset. Leaders and groups must look at each separate performance challenge they face, decide if they really need a performance unit, and then choose the best discipline for their situation. The two key disciplines are ways to achieve demanding performance results, not arbitrary names for types of groups.

TABLE 1.1 Effective group fundamentals versus the single-leader or team disciplines

Effective Work Group: That Interacts Well	Single-Leader Discipline: Performance Unit	Real-Team Discipline: Performance Unit
Clearly understood charter or purpose (not necessarily related to enterprise performance).	Strong performance charter and purpose comprised mostly of individual contributions.	Compelling performance challenge comprised of many collective work products.
Hierarchical leader promotes open communication and coordination.	Focused, single leader applies relevant experience and know-how to create performance focus.	Leadership role shifted/shared among members to reflect and exploit performance potential.
Individual goals seldom add up to a clear performance purpose for the group. The goals are not outcome-based.	Individual outcome-based goals and work products that add up to the performance purpose.	Outcome-based goals include both individual and collective work products (the latter predominates).
Clear roles and areas of responsibility remain constant throughout the group effort.	Stable roles and contributions reflect talents and skills of members.	Shifting roles and contributions to match varying performance tasks, as well as exploiting and developing member skills/talents.
Accountability is understood, but consequence management principles seldom prevail.	Individual accountability enforced primarily by leader; consequence management usually prevails.	Both individual and mutual accountability, largely peer- and self-enforced. However, only the team can "fail."

Linking Work Products to Performance

Whenever a small group can deliver performance through the combined sum of individual contributions, then the single-leader discipline is the most effective choice. This choice is fast, efficient, and comfortable, since most organizational units have followed the single-leader model for decades. However, if there must be collective contributions in addition to individual efforts, then the group should apply the team discipline. We choose to call such contributions work products. As illustrated in Figure 1.2, many group performance challenges can be achieved through the sum of individual work products. Other challenges demand the extra, team-based performance that arises from collective work products.

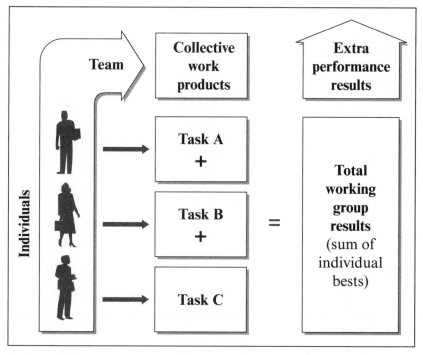

FIGURE 1.2 Collective work potential

Such products add an important dimension of performance that simply cannot be achieved primarily by individuals working on their own; hence, the value of the collective work product can be significant. The collective work product is the reason why teams outperform single-leader units.

Collective work products come from the hands-on work of two or more people, each with different skills, talents, and perspectives, who collaborate to produce value not achievable by any one of them alone. For example, a market researcher who collaborates with a product designer and a sales representative to design, set up, conduct, and debrief a focus group creates value from their joint or collective work effort. The skills, effort, and talent of all three combine to produce the focus group and what is to be learned from it. The different perspectives of the three people working together result in a better set of focus-group questions and interactions, as well as a richer interpretation of the response. If one of the three people conducts the focus group, or even if each of them conducts a separate focus group, the value of their merging perspectives would be largely lost.

A collective work product requires the skills, talents, and melded perspectives of several members of the group working together. One person working independently cannot produce the same quality product. Also, the leader cannot create the product by simply combining the individual work efforts of several people. Members have to roll up their sleeves and work together (either around the table, over the phone, or across the Internet). When performance demands collective-work products through real-time collaboration and integration of multiple skills and perspectives, the sum of individual work products and contributions falls short, and the single-leader approach will under-perform.

Individual work products come from individual effort, talent, and skill. Sounds obvious, and it is. The value created derives primarily from the hands-on work of one person. For example, a market researcher who designs, sets up, conducts, and debriefs a focus group by herself creates an individual work product. The researcher might ask an assistant to make phone calls, get help from an audio-visual technician in recording the focus group, or ask an editor to review the draft of the conclusions for clarity. But the researcher is doing the essential value-added work.

The distinction here is one of common sense. Yet, it is a distinction far too often ignored. In this case, four people are doing the work: the market researcher, the assistant, the technician, and the editor. However, most of the value in the work product from the focus group comes primarily from one person: the market researcher. It is the market researcher's individual work product. In the case of the jointly designed and conducted focus group in the preceding example, the collective interactions of the market researcher, the product designer, and the sales representative create the value.

People sometimes confuse work products with decisions. Work products, whether individual or collective, are more about work than decisions. Work products involve more than reviewing, deciding, and delegating—the actions so often associated with the job of manager. For example, steering committees that review, discuss, decide, and delegate are not producing collective work products. They are, as a committee, performing the classic management role of making decisions. But decisions—even though they often create value in and of themselves—are not the work products that define small group disciplines. The work leading to such decisions, as well as the work that such decisions require, may warrant performance unit levels of effort. Thus the decision event itself may dictate performance unit work. As a consequence, steering committees can seldom be classified as teams, although they may sponsor or stimulate group actions that warrant performance unit action.

In choosing between the single-leader and the team disciplines, groups must determine if their goals require significant and essential collective work products, or if the performance challenge is best achieved through the sum of individual work products and contributions. If the group cannot identify important, *required* collective work products, the team-approach should not be applied.

In the previous sentence, the word "*required*" is important. In our experience, most small groups can imagine many possibilities for collective work products. For example, the market researcher could easily approach the focus group in either of the ways described above. The key question, therefore, is not whether your group can imagine one or more meaningful and important collective work products, but whether the specific performance challenge at hand *requires* and benefits from collective work products.

Consider, then, these two examples of different performance challenges:

Challenge 1: "We need to know if our core consumer segments will respond favorably or unfavorably to emphasizing 'healthy' and 'natural' in our upcoming ad campaign."

Challenge 2: "We must understand if we can grow our customer base significantly by redesigning our product line that currently sells so well to the 'fifty-plus crowd' in ways that will appeal to people in their teens and twenties."

A market researcher could imagine approaching Challenge 1 through delivering the kind of collective work product described earlier. But, in our experience, performance does not necessarily require that approach. Neither product designers nor sales representatives are needed to assist the market researcher in designing, conducting, or learning from a series of focus groups whether 'healthy' and 'natural' will benefit or hurt sales. On the other hand, it is difficult to imagine anyone succeeding against Challenge 2 without collective work products. There are too many uncertainties and open questions, all of which would benefit significantly from the real-time combination of the differing skills, experiences, and perspectives of the market researcher, product designer, and sales representative.

EXERCISE 1.1
Learn From Your Own Experience

Gather one or more groups of people. Ask them to take a few minutes to write down at least one prior experience when they believed they were part of a really effective team versus one when they felt the group was ineffective. When everyone has completed this task, give them another five minutes to identify the characteristics that distinguished the two situations. Once people have completed this assignment, ask the whole group to divide itself into subgroups of four to eight people, with some groups focusing only on the characteristics of effective teams and others on the characteristics of ineffective teams. Give these groups twenty minutes to discuss their insights before asking each subgroup to share feedback with the whole group.

When you have gathered the feedback, ask the group to compare the findings and insights they have generated with the material in Chapter 1: (1) the five basic elements of all effective groups, (2) the team discipline, (3) the single-leader discipline, and (4) "compromise units."

EXERCISE 1.2
Test Your Understanding

Use the true/false test in Table 1.2 to evaluate your understanding of the two key disciplines and related concepts.

TABLE 1.2 Test your understanding

		True	False
1.	A team approach is better than a leader-led approach only if significant collective work products are needed.		
2.	A team approach is likely to be more effective than a leader-led effort when the number of members exceeds twenty-five.		
3.	In groups larger than twenty, the most practical way to achieve team levels of performance is to utilize subgroups.		
4.	Leader-led groups achieve results faster than teams.		
5.	Once a team has mastered the basics, their results are just as fast as a leader-led group.		
6.	At the start of a project, it is important for every small group to decide to be a team and then figure out how best to adhere to that discipline.		
7.	A small group can sometimes function as a team and sometimes as a single leader unit, provided the group applies the right discipline in the right places at the right times.		
8.	The best way for a group to achieve team levels of performance is for the formal leader to back off and empower the group to manage itself.		
9.	Teaming is nothing more than getting along and helping each other.		
10.	People in groups will only respect decisions if they are made by the boss.		
11.	Sometimes my group will perform best if the leader will just make decisions, assign each of us our individual jobs, and just get on with it.		
12.	Most people are more comfortable with clearly defined responsibilities and roles, as well as individual accountability.		
13.	Teaming is required whenever it is possible to imagine any collective work product.		
14.	Teams typically set higher standards and goals than what the chain of command expects.		
15.	Clear and compelling performance goals are what create great teams, instead of the desire to team up.		

Answers: 1. T; 2. F; 3. T; 4. T; 5. T; 6. F; 7. T; 8. F; 9. F; 10. F; 11. T; 12. T; 13. F; 14. T; 15. T

EXERCISE 1.3
Assess and React

Gather your group together. Ask each person to answer the questions in Table 1.3 on a 1 to 5 scale, with 1 being *strongly agree,* and 5 indicating *strongly disagree.* When you have completed your answers, compare notes. Discuss whether your group balances the single-leader discipline with the team discipline, or perhaps habitually uses only one of these disciplines. Also, discuss whether your group is a compromise unit. Finally, ask yourselves whether there are any specific performance challenges your group faces that would benefit from a different approach from the one usually taken.

TABLE 1.3 Assess and react

		1	2	3	4	5
1.	Our working approach is determined by the way in which the leader assigns tasks and runs the meetings.					
2.	We hold one another accountable for higher collective results than our leaders and sponsors expect of us.					
3.	We all participate in evaluating each other's efforts instead of leaving that up to our leader.					
4.	Most members of our group are not comfortable in leading the group.					
5.	Members of our group are very clear about their roles, and we maintain those roles in all meetings and interactions.					
6.	We need clearer decisions and less time spent on touchy-feely stuff.					
7.	Most of the real work required is best done by each member working on his/her assignment in his/her area of competence.					
8.	We spend a lot of time between meetings collaborating on work that couldn't get done individually.					
9.	Our leader delegates effectively to others and only supervises and monitors individual progress.					
10.	When we set our goals, we seldom distinguish between individual goals and joint or collective goals.					

TABLE 1.3 *continued*

		1	2	3	4	5
11.	We learn a lot from one another because we often shift roles and share work tasks.					
12.	We seldom take time to discuss and decide on our purpose and aspirations as a group; these are clearly specified by our leader.					
13.	When new members of our group are added, we spend quality time as a group incorporating their views into our purpose, goals, and working approach.					
14.	All of our meetings are conducted very efficiently by the leader, and the topics and agendas are clear in advance.					
15.	It is more important that we get along with one another than achieve extraordinary results.					
16.	All members of the group feel comfortable suggesting changes in the group's goals and working approach.					
17.	Our group is too big to function effectively as a team; hence, most of the real work is done by individual and subgroups, only some of which work as performance teams.					
18.	We are each held accountable by the leader for individual goals and contributions that add to our group's purpose.					
19.	Time is clearly more important to our purpose than collective work products; hence, most of the work is individually driven.					
20.	Members are primarily respected by the others for their skills rather than personality.					

EXERCISE 1.4
Match Your Performance Challenges To The Two disciplines

Gather your group and spend whatever time is needed to list the most pressing performance challenges that you currently face. Refine this list until you have five to ten particular challenges. Pick one challenge from the list. Review Figure 1.1 and Table 1.1. Now, ask half of your group to make the best possible arguments in favor of applying the single-leader discipline to the selected performance challenge. Ask the other half of the group to argue in favor of the team discipline. When you have completed this debate, move on to a second specific challenge from your list, then a third, and so on.

EXERCISE 1.5
Does Performance Require Collective Work Products?

Again, start by identifying one or more specific performance challenges facing your group. Pick one of those challenges to discuss. Ask the group to brainstorm regarding the kind of work that must get done to succeed. Convert this description of work into a series of specific work products. Identify and discuss among yourselves whether the work products are individual or collective. Then, using Figure 1.2, discuss whether your group's performance *requires* or benefits from collective work products. Remember that the question here is not whether you can identify collective work products, or whether any particular collective work product is a good idea or potentially valuable. Instead, the question is whether the performance objectives and goals demand such work products.

CHAPTER 2

Virtual Teaming

Working together apart . . .

Does your team include members who must work together from separate physical locations across different time zones? If yes, then it is likely you need "virtual team" capability, both human and technological. To some extent, virtual teaming has always been with us. For example, groups have long used teleconferencing to connect team members whose logistical constraints precluded their physical presence at a key work session. Increasingly, however, virtual teaming is becoming an integral part of most small group work, primarily as a consequence of technology that has evolved way beyond mere teleconferencing. Today, organizations are no longer confined to team efforts that assemble people from the same location or the same time zone. Indeed, small groups of people from two or more locations and time zones routinely convene for collaborative purposes. Such groups are expected to take advantage of hardware such as intranets, Internet, video and teleconferencing, and fax, as well as software that supports activities like project management, document sharing, and executive management information synthesis. For purposes of this book, we categorize all such technologies, both hardware and software, as *groupwork technology,* or more simply, *groupware.*

The growing diversity and capacity of groupware help make virtual teaming possible and practical, if not inevitable. But technology alone does not explain the rapid rise in virtual teaming. As people-intensive sources of competitive advantage have gained importance, organizations, from commercial to government to nonprofit, have shifted how and where work is done. In short, the workplace of today is a far cry from the assembly lines and offices of yesteryear. In fact, twenty years ago, most work done by people in organizations was a function of routine processes dictated by formal structures, rules, and programs. Today, a lot of work still reflects such formal elements but just as often work occurs in the context of more flexible, ad hoc, and nonroutine special projects.

Project work has become as important to the success of organizations as process work. Short- to medium-term efforts that seek performance improvements in many different arenas, such as quality, customer care, reengineering, product development, strategy formulation, and innovation, consume more labor than ever before. Such projects are usually staffed by small groups of people who apply a constantly changing mix of the team and single-leader disciplines.

The many challenges that require project work has increased the *demand* for work done in small groups. At the same time, technology has increased the *supply* of project workers because organizations are not limited to workers located in the same place or time zone. If, for example, you were asked to assemble a group to tackle a significant strategic alliance project, you would not need to limit your choices to people located in the same building as yourself. Instead, you and your organization could select people from among your company's various facilities throughout the world. In fact, you could staff your small group with people who are not even part of your company, such as outside experts, special researchers, and alliance partner resources. Consequently, if your headquarters, plant, or office complex houses two-hundred people, but your company, its critical alliance partners, and professional advisors number in the thousands, the choices for your effort are vastly expanded.

Of the dozens of teams we researched during the writing of *The Wisdom of Teams,* only a handful had membership from multiple locations. By contrast, in the decade since publishing the book, we have witnessed an explosion in the number of such teams. Virtual teaming efforts now pervade all kinds of organizations and institutions. Yet, this phenomenon is only part of a much more fundamental change, the rapidly expanding amount of *virtual work.*

Virtual work consists of tasks and activities that occur within today's vast network of electronics, telecommunications, and information technology. The computer, with all its attendant software and hardware, continues to redefine where and how work is done. Even co-located, non-virtual teams, where all members work down the hall from one another, increasingly interact over the same technology as virtual teams. This technology makes all communication quicker and easier. As a result, the vast majority of office workers rely on user-friendly computers, e-mail, project management, document sharing, and other software. Therefore, even co-workers *literally sitting next to one another in the same team room* will have many virtual moments, interacting and collaborating through groupware. Groupwork technology permits interactions to take place within time frames that fit the convenience and different work patterns of workers.

In short, small groups increasingly work virtually even when not involved in virtual teams. Their work across a crowded room through the medium of computers is similar to the work of virtual teams using computers across larger spans of time and geography. In each case, the groups face the challenge of making the best use of groupware in their continuing efforts to deliver performance in new and different ways.

Virtual Teaming: Same Disciplines in New Context

Not surprisingly, virtual work and teaming efforts pose challenges that differ markedly from co-located work. (See Chapter 8 for further discussion of these challenges.) None of the challenges, however, are as significant as what we believe to be the most critical issue: Are the two disciplines that are essential for small group performance—team and single-leader—different for virtual teams?

Our answer is, "No." The two disciplines are the same for virtual and non-virtual teams, as well as for virtual and non-virtual work. Having participated in, observed, and reviewed dozens of virtual teams over many years, we remain convinced that choosing and applying the right discipline is the most significant difference between the virtual groups who deliver performance versus those that fall short. To validate this belief, as well as expand our range of examples for this book, we worked with associates from Katzenbach Partners LLC to research the efforts of over a dozen virtual teams from different industries and global dispersions.

The results of this research were not surprising, but they did convince us that the world of virtual teaming deserves special attention. Fortunately, some of the most effective teams reviewed during our work on *The Wisdom of Teams* were virtual teams. For example, the McKinsey Rapid Response Team members were located in Atlanta, New York, and San Francisco. The Rapid Response Team faced challenges in applying the team discipline that differed in important ways from those confronted by physically co-located teams. For example, the Rapid Response Team could not have performed as well without spending time in face-to-face meetings. The time together toward the beginning of the effort and again when critical issues or challenges required face-to-face meeting was of particular value to the team. But basic team discipline consisting of a small number of people with complementary skills holding themselves mutually accountable to a common purpose, common performance goals, and commonly agreed upon working approach, did not change. Nor did the three litmus tests for identifying when to use the team discipline: (1) performance goals that demanded collective work products, (2) shifting member and leadership roles, and (3) mutual plus individual accountability. These imperatives stand the tests of time, distance, and technology.

Over the years, we have observed that virtual groups, relying on the single-leader discipline, succeed when that discipline is the best choice. The research provided current evidence of our initial hypotheses, and expanded our insights about how virtual groups work differently in applying the appropriate discipline, single-leader or real-team. In one of many examples, a small group of managers at KPMG Peat Marwick was asked to oversee the move of hundreds of people from one building to another. This building transition group relied heavily on e-mail, document sharing, simple project management, and other collaboration software. While the members of the group practiced good teamwork behavior, such as effective communications, sharing of best practices, and mutual support, they relied primarily on the single-leader discipline. The group leader was in control: making the critical decisions, allocating individual tasks and responsibility, facilitating group communications, evaluating and monitoring task progress, and holding people accountable for individual contributions. Under the group leader's command and with the contributions of the individuals involved, the group met all the performance challenges they faced—and their use of groupwork technology helped a lot.

In contrast, when virtual teams misapply, confuse, or lose sight of the two basic disciplines, they fail. For example, a group of five people from Boston and New York were charged with designing and delivering a key feature in a suite of software products. These five people had the necessary programming, software architecture, business knowledge, and marketing skills. Success clearly warranted the team discipline because collective work products, mutual accountability, and shared leadership were essential in achieving the group's performance purpose. Instead, the group relied on the single-leader approach, and, consequently, fell short of their goal. This software group and the KPMG building transition group actually used the same groupware. In fact, the software group's expertise and familiarity with the technology far exceeded that of the building transition group. Therefore, it is the choice of discipline, and not the software, that matters.

Our point is simple: *Technology is an enabler of both disciplines, not a substitute for either.* With respect to groupwork technology, it does not matter whether groups are comprised of novices or experts. The basics of small-group performance remain the same. You must learn when to use the single-leader discipline to achieve your goals and when to use the team discipline. Leading-edge technology, no matter how well applied, will not compensate for choosing the wrong discipline, or applying it poorly.

Indeed, this was the central conclusion reached by KPMG, following experimentation with groupware among several teams. The small group that oversaw the building move successfully used the technology to enable the single-leader discipline. Other groups also succeeded in using the technology to support the team discipline. Yet, not surprisingly, every single group who fell into the trap of hoping that the groupware would substitute for managerial discipline failed.

If your small group must do virtual work, the most important lesson in this book is that of choosing and using the discipline that fits your particular performance need. You cannot rely on technology, any more than you can natural instinct, for making the appropriate choice. In both disciplines, technology can help the work, but it cannot replace using the right discipline at the right time and place. So, focus clearly on your performance challenges and learn when and how best to use the team or single-leader approach. Do not assume that the basic disciplines of performance will fit merely because you are employing advanced technology or specially designed groupware. And do not make the mistake of assuming that technology will somehow provide the necessary discipline.

Groupwork Technology: Key Features and Functionality

A variety of groupwork technologies now permit you to collaborate with others across different time zones and in different places. As noted earlier, some of these technologies have been around for decades, for example, fax, telephone, teleconferencing, and video conferencing. Other groupware has emerged in the past decade with the growing use of computers and the Internet, including e-mail and various collaboration, project management, and software applications. There are hundreds of technological options from which to choose.

This section introduces the most relevant and important features and discusses how virtual teams can take advantage of them. Specific obstacles and difficulties posed by the technology are discussed in Chapter 8.

1. *Video, chatroom, and teleconferencing* devices permit groups who are not in the same location or time zones to hold meetings and discussions. Those who have used this type of groupware already know how this experience differs when contrasted with face-to-face meetings. In chatrooms and teleconferencing, there is no body language or facial expressions to help interpret meaning and intent; in video conferencing, the sound and image can include awkward hesitations. Jokes, for example, are often difficult to follow because of the pauses. Groups quickly learn that all three technologies work best when the interactions are confined to need-to-know information or issues that everyone must understand and resolve together. As one person with experience in virtual teaming told us, "Using these technologies just to get status reports from each individual is really boring and a waste of time." Participants also recognize that establishing some working rules or etiquette norms up front helps ensure better interactions and minimizes the discourteous behavior of not paying attention. For example, people using this technology instead of face-to-face meetings often find it easier to tune out (one popular form of tuning out is when a presumed participant is actually doing other work). Finally, many groups have learned how to use two of these technologies simultaneously: chatroom, plus either video or teleconferencing. By doing so, people within the group can choose to express them-

selves by speaking or in writing, an option that often produces both richer discussions and input and dialogues with fewer interruptions. Why? Because when only one means of communication is available, people compete for the floor. When two means are available, people can log in their comments without disrupting the flow of conversation.

2. *Email:* The good news and bad news about e-mail are increasingly well known and obvious. Used well, e-mail permits members of groups to communicate critical information, challenges, and issues. But without careful attention to when and how to rely on e-mail, groups add to the proliferation of e-mail that increasingly is the bane of so many. Worst of all, carelessly composed e-mail messages can insult, embarrass, and alienate receivers. More subtly, e-mail is a poor substitute for the following threaded discussions feature described below. Groups who rely on e-mail instead of threaded discussions encounter more frustration than progress in raising, discussing, and resolving issues critical to the performance of the group. As one person told us, "When I read a lengthy e-mail, it sparks hundreds of thoughts and questions. But unlike in face-to-face team meetings, I can't ask them or engage in a discussion about them."

3. *Threaded discussions* permit groups to raise, discuss, and resolve issues in orderly, comprehensible, and controlled ways. They work as follows: Let's say I raise Issue A and post it to the team. You respond to my comment. I respond back to your comment. A third member of our team responds to my original comment. And a fourth member of the team responds to your response to my

EXHIBIT 2.1 Threaded discussions

When you log on to your team's groupware, this is what you see:

Issue A (raised by me)
   Your response to Issue A
     My response to your response
     Fourth team member's response to your response
    Third team member's response to Issue A
Issue B (raised by fourth team member)

original comment. Finally, the fourth member of our team raises a completely different issue, Issue B. Exhibit 2.1 shows what each of the members of our team sees when they use their mouse to click on this threaded discussion. As you can see, anyone can follow the discussion from start to finish and, in doing so, see who is responding to whom and what is being said about each issue. Threaded discussions, then, offer the opportunity for teams to create and record a repository and history of their thinking and work. Used wisely, this feature of groupwork is invaluable to teams.

4. *Document management* provides teams a library for their written and visual work. Reports, presentations, brochures, memos, training materials, sales materials —any document can be stored and accessed by members of the team. Moreover, team members can check documents out of the library and return modified documents. As long as the software includes version control, teams can be assured that no version of the document is ever lost. Consequently, if I modify your draft, and, later, the team decides your draft was better or

wants to access it for other reasons, your unmodified version remains easily retrievable.

5. *People profiles,* background information, skill and experience descriptions, contact information, calendars, roles, responsibilities, and tasks can be stored using groupwork technology. While this information can be retained in paper files, the ease of access, extraction, and modification is often enhanced by well-designed groupware.

6. *Metrics and goals* can be posted. Moreover, the group can track progress, directly or by linking the groupwork software to other information systems in the company. Metrics and goals can be modified without losing the initial version. Most important, the technology can help enforce discipline and ensure outcome-based goals by tracking the groups progress against those goals.

7. *Project management* starts with project definition. Our group can define our project in terms of purpose and goals. As we progress, we can subdivide the project into subprojects, as well as tasks. Each of these tasks, including the deadlines and metrics, can be assigned to members of our group. Moreover, we can use project management software to identify which subprojects and tasks are most critical and dependent on one another. By understanding such interdependencies, we can establish the most efficient and effective overall project plan and timeline for completion. We can also subdivide goals into individual and collective work products, ensuring team effort in the right places. If we are disciplined, we can also differentiate subprojects to fit team or single-leader approaches.

8. *Groupwork technology can provide executive/management information:* who in the group is getting their work done on time, who participates in threaded discussions; who read or provided input to critical documents, and what progress is being made toward goals, metrics, and other milestones. Thus, leaders can more readily pinpoint members who need special attention and what type of attention is appropriate.

EXERCISE 2.1
Are You A Virtual Team? Will You Do Significant Virtual Work? So What?

Consider the members of your group; that is, the people who must work together to achieve some performance purpose and challenge. Are a significant number located in different locations and time zones? If so, you warrant virtual team consideration. Even if you are not a virtual team, will you do significant amounts of virtual work? That is, will it benefit you to interact routinely with one another through the medium of groupware?

If you are a virtual team or will do significant amounts of virtual work, you should take time out to discuss the implications of how virtual teaming and work compare with normal, co-located efforts.

EXERCISE 2.2
What Groupware Technology Will You Use?

If you are a virtual team or will do significant amounts of virtual work, discuss and decide which of the basic features of groupwork technology shown in Table 2.1 you plan to use on a regular basis.

TABLE 2.1 Groupwork technology

	Regularly	Once in A While	Never
Videoconferencing			
Teleconferencing			
Chatroom			
E-mail			
Threaded discussions			
Document management			
People profiles and contact			
Metrics and goals			
Project management			
Executive/management information			
Other: _____			

EXERCISE 2.3
Novices and/or Experts: Personal Experiences/Best Practices with Groupware

Once you have selected the groupware features and functions you plan to utilize, take an hour or two with your group to discuss your individual knowledge and experience levels with each feature. Are you novices or experts? What best practices do you know from personal experience? If, as a group, you have few to no members with deep expertise, how will you obtain relevant skills or assistance? What specific expectations will you set for learning and using the features you have selected? If, on the other hand, most or all of you have relevant experience, how will you avoid misunderstandings and miscommunications as you move forward?

If you cannot meet face-to-face to have this discussion,

you should use features such as videoconferencing or threaded discussion for the same purpose.

EXERCISE 2.4
Practice, Practice, Practice: Threaded Discussion

For each feature you select, design an initial experiment in
which all members can practice using the feature as well as
deliver on a specific set of expectations. For example, use
threaded discussions. Pick an issue facing your team and,
over a set period of time, such as two days, use the threaded
discussion feature to dialogue and interact with one another
about that issue. Any issue will do. For example, you might
conduct Exercise 1.5, about collective work products, through
the medium of a threaded discussion. *Require all members to
participate in this discussion.* At the end of the two-day trial,
have a follow-up discussion about what worked, what didn't,
and the implications of future group use of threaded discussions. Again, you should design and conduct a similar exercise for each separate feature your group intends to utilize.

EXERCISE 2.5
Practice, Practice, Practice: Conferencing Plus Chat

Schedule a teleconference or videoconference call. Arrange
for everyone attending to log on to the team's chatroom. Pick
an issue you would like to discuss. Appoint someone as mod-
erator and someone else to monitor the input to the chatroom. Set the expectation that each person will experiment
with two different ways of providing input to the discussion:
(1) by speaking and (2) by typing in comments to the chatroom feature. When your group has thoroughly discussed the

issue at hand, turn the attention of the group to debriefing what worked, what didn't, and the implications of using these combined features of groupware.

EXERCISE 2.6
Practice, Practice, Practice: Document Management

Agree about the use of the document management feature of your groupware technology. Make sure each person is familiar with the application's rules regarding checking out, modifying, reposting, and checking in documents, as well as saving distinct versions of each document. Once you have familiarized yourselves with the application, select a document that is important to the work of your group. Assign someone the job of creating and posting the document in your relevant groupware application. Mandate that every person in the group experiment with checking out, modifying, and reposting the document, as well as helping to ensure that the group saves each distinct version of the document. Assign a limited time frame for this experiment; we suggest one week. At the end of the week, discuss what worked, what didn't, and the implications of making the best use of document management as you move forward.

EXERCISE 2.7
Customize Training

If your group chooses to get training on groupware technology, work diligently with the trainer or facilitator to customize the training, so that:

1. You are trained only on those features and functions you will regularly use.

2. You have the discussion included in Exercise 2.3 as part of the training.

3. The training includes a hands-on version of Exercises 2.4, 2.5, 2.6, or similar exercises for other features and functions.

4. The training includes "next steps" discussions and agreements about how your group will and will not use the various groupware features emphasized.

CHAPTER 3

Outcomes—Not Activities—Shape Your Choice

You have to know what success looks like . . .

The core message in Chapter 1 is *make conscious choices.* Small-group effectiveness starts with consciously choosing which performance challenges are best suited to the team discipline and which warrant the single-leader discipline. Chapter 2 argues that virtual teams and non-virtual teams must make the same basic choices. To reiterate, the two approaches to small-group performance are not arbitrary names for labeling groups themselves: they are two distinct management disciplines. Groups should not choose to "be a team" or "be a single-leader group" based upon personal preference, an executive mandate, or the misperception that one discipline always works better than the other. Instead, groups seeking to optimize performance should base the selection of discipline on the requirements of the performance situation or task at hand. The best performing groups excel at integrating both disciplines.

In this chapter, we focus on gaining clarity and rigor in your articulation and understanding of performance. *In our experience, the more specifically small groups describe and characterize their performance challenges and goals, the better they are at making the best choice between the team and single-leader disciplines.* For example, a small group in an e-commerce company, seeking to improve the experience of users on the company web-site, will have a more productive discussion about the team versus the single-leader discipline with regard to Performance Statement 1 than Performance Statement 2:

Performance Statement 1: Reduce average user access time from 5.9 seconds to 1.5 seconds within six weeks.

Performance Statement 2: Figure out ways to improve the user experience of our web site.

Both of these statements offer compelling challenges. And, Performance Statement 2 might better resemble the charter or purpose statement with which many small groups begin their journey to success. In fact, Performance Statement 1 represents one of several distinct performance challenges within the overall aspiration captured by Statement 2, making our point: To achieve significant performance results, groups must convert broad aspirations, such as Performance Statement 2, into specific performance goals and objectives, as in Performance Statement 1, so that the groups are in the position to decide when to apply the team discipline or when the single-leader discipline would work best.

When small groups lose sight of their performance rationale, they fall prey to personality conflicts, poor communications, and bad feelings. Too often, they reach out for soft-side facilitators or fall back on bonding exercises that seldom work. It is sufficiently difficult to resolve subjective and messy issues, even with the aid of clear, compelling performance goals to guide the group. But without such goals, groups become rudderless; and, neither facilitation nor bonding nor leader exhortation can replace the missing focus on performance. Instead, the standards for resolution typically become hierarchy, power, personality, favoritism, and other troubling and divisive criteria.

The most troublesome misstep down this path occurs when leaders view the purpose of collaboration in terms of *activities rather outcomes*. Organizations make this mistake over and over again, e.g.:

1. Enterprise visions emphasize becoming a "team-based organization" without reference to what that means or why it matters, i.e., *the team's the thing!*

2. Change initiatives stress the number of teams created as the measure of their success. If you are not a member of a team, you somehow feel guilty! Everyone claims team affiliation, i.e., *more is better!*

3. Team training programs become mired down as every aspect of empowerment, feelings, and togetherness is explored. Content centers on team building and bonding. Trainers simply assume that participants understand the connection between such exercises and work, i.e., *empowerment is what it's all about!*

4. Culture change efforts highlight the values of team and teamwork in the absence of any link to specific goals or challenges. Well-intended leaders perpetuate the notion that teamwork (certainly an admirable value) will somehow lead to team performance (a rigorous discipline), i.e., *creating a team environment becomes an objective in itself!*

In each of these cases, the performance foundation for why groups must team is obscure, and disappointment, frustration, and wasted effort are the inevitable results. The people involved assume that teaming is necessary and good: a lazy assumption that leads to trouble. When there is no rationale behind teaming, people act as though there is no distinction between the two disciplines. This quickly leads to compromise units: small groups who do not effectively apply the team discipline or the single-leader discipline. To avoid this trap, groups must work hard to clarify, specify, and enrich their understanding and articulation of performance, as well as the outcomes and metrics that determine success.

Articulating Outcome-Based Performance Goals

We urge you to articulate and then use *outcome-based goals* instead of *activity-based goals* in making your choice between team and single-leader disciplines. (For a complete discussion of using outcome-based goals as the foundation for managing performance and change throughout an organization, see Doug Smith's book entitled *Make Success Measurable!* Another Mindbook/Workbook.) As the terms imply, outcome-based goals describe the specific outcomes by which success will be determined, while activity-based goals describe the activities believed necessary to achieve that success. Outcomes are the results, consequences, end products, or impacts of actions. You can usually see, sometimes touch, and always do something with them: they are clearly identifiable and frequently tangible. Outcomes can be measured in different ways, including time, speed, cost, revenue, profit, defects, errors, volume, and number, among others. In the system for Marriott International Hotels, for example, one of the most critical measurable outcomes for all employees is the scores of their Guest Service Index. Each month that index reports highly credible customer feedback and is calibrated to reflect both individual and team efforts. Whatever the measurement, outcomes answer the question, "How would you know success?" for the challenge at hand.

The following are examples of outcome-based goals:

1. Win three new accounts in the next quarter.

2. Reduce the average duration of patient-days by one day over the next five months.

3. Halve the time it takes to process and approve new software licenses by March 30.

4. Improve the retention rate among top-rated performers by 20% this year without incurring any additional salary or benefit expense.

5. Convert at least half of our franchisees to company-owned stores this year, while simultaneously improving store-based service quality scores among company-owned stores by twofold.

6. Triple the number of product line extensions brought to market over the next six months.

7. Within six weeks, eliminate the top three causes of customer-defined defects on our automated voice response system, while decreasing the average response time by at least half.

8. Raise first-round venture capital financing by October without giving up more than 30% of the company.

In contrast to outcome-based goals, activity-based goals describe the activities and actions at the heart of the performance challenge in question. For the preceding series of examples, the following illustrate activity-based goal statements:

1. Develop a plan for winning new accounts.

2. Save money through reducing patient days.

3. Reengineer the new software license process.

4. Make this company the best place to work.

5. Implement our new customer quality strategy through company-owned stores.

6. Build a culture of innovation.

7. Improve customer service by fixing the automated response system.

8. Find the investors we need.

Look closely at the difference between the activity-based goals and outcome-based goals. When goals are stated as activities, small groups have a difficult time determining which performance discipline is required. Is it necessary to have real-time collaboration? How do we benefit from the integration of multiple skills through shifting roles and shared leadership, collective work products, and mutual accountability? Activity-based goals make it extremely difficult to articulate whether the sum of individual-best contributions will produce the appropriate results. Outcome-based goals facilitate purposeful group dialogue. You can more easily explore whether individual contributions will deliver the required results versus the collective contributions that come from collaboration, shifting roles, shared leadership, and collective work products.

Unfortunately, with the exception of revenue and cost goals, most goal statements in organizations are activity-based. Most annual plans, personal performance plans, project or initiative plans, and other forms of goal commitments feature statements such as "research what customers want," "develop a strategy for hiring," "improve communications," "build a market-driven culture," and "reorganize into teams." There may or may not be dates attached to these goals. But even if accompanied by dates, activity-based goals never answer the question, "How would we know we succeeded?" Instead, activity-based goals assume the pursuit of the given activity will somehow create the desired results.

Answering the question "How will you know success?" is one of the most powerful ways your group can convert activity-based goals into outcome-based goals (see Exercise 3.2). Think, for example, about the common desire to improve communications. How would we know we succeeded? If we answer, "We will know we have improved communications when communications improve," all of us would laugh. Another good test is whether the obverse of a goal statement sounds foolish (e.g., "get worse at communications"). Such absurdity is a good sign that activities, instead of outcomes, are being discussed. In this example, success has more to do with performance results that currently elude us because of poor communication.

Perhaps we are falling short in customer satisfaction because we permit engineers and technologists to design and build products that result in significant numbers of customer complaints. We may choose to reverse that trend *by seeking to reduce customer complaints on our four most critical product lines by 20% by the year's end*. We intend to succeed by asking engineers, technologists, customer service representatives, and marketing and sales to communicate more effectively with one another about customer product needs. Such communication could result in a reworking of the new product or

EXHIBIT 3.1 Activities lead to outcomes

The activity, "improve communications"→ leads to → the activity of "better understanding customer's product needs" → leads to → the activity of "reengineering the new product development process → leads to → an outcome of "better products in shorter time" → which can be expressed as a specific outcome-based goal such as: "By year's end, reduce customer complaints by at least 20% through the introduction of new products in our four main product categories."

product line extension process to increase both the quality of current products and the flow of new products to the markets. At the same time, we seek to reduce the number, frequency, and response time of customer complaints. In each case, we are trying to accomplish specific outcomes that matter to customers, instead of merely improving communications for the sake of improving communications.

Exhibit 3.1 maps the various activities in this example to desired outcomes. You will note that improved communications is an activity that we must get better at as part of reworking or reengineering the new product process. Reworking the new product process is also an activity we must pursue in order to deliver outcome-based performance results measured by more new products, as well as a reduced number of customer complaints. These activities are necessary to success; but unlike outcomes, activities are not a good set of goals for success. Outcomes are.

The discipline of team basics is itself an activity. So is the single-leader discipline. Just as improving communications and reengineering might produce outcomes that matter, so can teams and single-leader units. But, as demonstrated in

Exhibit 3.1, it rarely helps groups to set activities as goals. While being a team might help with group cohesion, being a team rarely serves as a useful performance goal.

Make Your Outcome-Based Goals SMART

To ensure your group is working with outcome-based goals, use the five criteria in the SMART acronym:[1]

1. *Specific:* Goals are specific when they answer what the group seeks to get better at and for whose benefit. The more specific the goal, the better. For example, in the preceding illustration with respect to new accounts, the group wants to improve new accounts. Yet, that example could be even more specific by describing the kind of new accounts. Instead of three new accounts, the goal might specify three new accounts in the emerging web-based business sector that demand alliance-based sales effort.

   When groups clearly specify what kind of work, process, or effort they hope to improve, as well as who will benefit from the effort, they make better choices. They become clearer about the extent to which collective work products versus individual best performances are required. Outcomes can be categorized as collective or individual work products, whereas activities cannot. In this example, a small group from two or more alliance partners could easily answer why the team discipline was needed to get better at alliance-based sales to new web-based business accounts. Without the collective effort of people with different skill-sets and from differ-

1. See *Make Success Measurable* by Douglas K. Smith.

ent companies, the group would be unlikely to succeed. Indeed, merely assigning one individual from each company the task of signing up more new accounts would probably fail because each individual would lack the full skills and experience required to demonstrate to customers the value of a combined offering. In contrast, if the goal were to "acquire three new accounts for our traditional line of grocery products," the sales group is likely to find that the single-leader discipline with strong individual accountability's sufficient for success, since all members of the group are equally knowledgeable in the traditional product offering.

2. *Measurable:* Goals are measurable when they provide the yardstick for evaluating success and answering the question, "By how much?" Every performance challenge uses one or more of the following four categories of success measurement:

   ■ *Time/speed:* This measures the time or speed it takes something to happen or be completed. Note that such measures might reflect a customer expectation (for example, customer service calls answered in less than one second), or indicate the amount of effort or investment demanded (for example, no more than five person-months of project effort).

   ■ *Cost:* This measures the cost of an input or activity as well as the investment required for a new product, capital, project, strategy, or other major purpose.

   ■ *Quality in terms of customer-defined defects or errors:* This measures how well products or services compare with company-imposed specifications (for example, there will never be more than four customers in any check-out line) or customer expectations (we will never have more than ten customer complaints per month, regardless of what the complaint is because the customer is always right). Most often, the number or frequency of defects, errors, or failures is used here.

■ *Positive yields:* This is a miscellaneous and large category that reflects positive expressions of what your group is attempting to accomplish. It typically includes financial metrics such as revenue, profit, or return on investment, as well as nonfinancial metrics such as number of new products or services, number of new or retained key hires, customer satisfaction, employee satisfaction, and so forth.

As your group considers each of these four categories, notice that the first two, time and cost, measure the effort or input required to produce some output that is best measured by one or both of the second two: quality or positive yields. Often, the best goals contain measurable improvements in productivity, that is, more output for less input. For example, "within 6 weeks, eliminate the top three causes of customer-defined defects on our automated voice response system, while decreasing the average response time by at least half" contains an improved output, reduced defects, plus a reduced amount of input and average speed. In addition, this goal statement answers the all-important question, "By how much?"

Metrics aid in the choice between the two disciplines. When the chosen metrics fit their performance challenges and convert to measurable goals, small groups usually find it easier to choose between team and single-leader disciplines. For example, in the preceding automated voice response goal, someone in the group might know about an off-the-shelf technology solution that could dramatically reduce response time without any extensive training or other change. If so, that challenge could best be solved using the single-leader discipline. On the other hand, the group might lack any good ideas about how to deliver the promised performance beyond getting customer service representatives and others to do a lot of team-based problem solving and improvement.

3. *Aggressive yet achievable:* The most effective goals make us aim high. Only by creating challenging goals will we get the most out of our capabilities. Aiming high applies to both individual and team goals. Yet, goals must also be credible if we expect people to persist. For example, a hospital that has incurred one to two million dollar deficits on a budget of one hundred million for five straight years could hardly expect to produce a twenty million dollar surplus in the coming year, without some dramatic windfall. Setting such a goal certainly would qualify as aggressive; it would also be unachievable. A leadership team might lay claim to such a goal, but most people throughout the institution would find it overly demanding, if not absurd, and soon give up trying. If, by contrast, the leadership team set a goal to reach breakeven or create a small surplus, team members and people throughout the institution would likely see the goal as both aggressive and achievable.

4. *Relevant:* Goals and metrics should directly relate to the challenge at hand. This sounds simple enough, but far too often, people set goals, particularly financial goals,

that only measure success indirectly or over extended time frames. Decades of orientation toward revenue, costs, profits, and investments have caused most people in most organizations to quickly settle on financial goals as the standard for success against all challenges. Yet, over the past fifteen to twenty years, we have witnessed a profusion of challenges that do not translate directly into dollars and cents. Such aspirations as time to market, reengineering, war for talent, customer service, and customer-defined quality usually do not lend themselves to direct or near-term financial measurement. While favorable economic results *lag* achievement against these challenges, the connections are not obvious. Hence, the best, most direct, and relevant goals and metrics for such efforts are better expressed with non-financial yardsticks. For example, speed, time, defects, errors, and user satisfaction are not financial, but they do measure performance results. Groups should spend time trying to articulate goals and metrics that directly track achieving the challenge at hand, rather than adhering to financial metrics that lag or are only indirectly indicative of performance. The more direct and relevant the metrics and goals selected, the more productive the feedback when the group reviews what is working, what is not working, and how to do better.

5. *Time-bound:* Goals without deadlines or milestones are not goals. They may be aspirations, values, and visions; but, they are not goals. By committing ourselves to a time frame, we ensure focus and accountability. And, to the extent that the overall time frame can be interspersed with milestones that track progress, so much the better.

Often, the selected time frame determines which discipline to use. Sometimes accelerated time pressures create an imperative for team performance. For example, consider the new software licensing process mentioned earlier. The stated goal was to cut the time of licensing in half by March 30. If a small group of lawyers, accountants, and sales managers set this goal ten or eleven months ahead of March 30, they could probably achieve the goal through the sum of their individual contributions since they would have plenty of time to work separately on individual pieces which could be integrated sequentially by the leader. However, if they set the goal only one month ahead, that is, on March 1 of the year in question, the shorter time frame for achievement could make the team discipline an imperative as the only way to ensure simultaneous collective efforts by all members rather than relying on sequential integration by the leader.

Most of the time, however, the single-leader discipline is faster because an experienced leader "knows best" how to proceed and need not spend much time bringing the group up-to-speed in shaping goals, working approach, and milestones. Between the single-leader and team disciplines, however, time frame can be a two-edged sword. On the one hand, most groups will operate much more efficiently in single-leader mode, particularly those with an experienced leader or with members who are unfamiliar or unpracticed at the team discipline. They will certainly accomplish individual work product results faster and with less bother. Consequently, many groups choose the single-leader discipline because "they don't want to waste time becoming a team."

On the other hand, this time efficiency comes with a limitation: the single-leader discipline will not produce the extra performance of teams. If that extra performance demands moving slower at first, then so be it. Most teams, by the way, work just as fast as single-leader groups once the team discipline has been mastered.

Armed with SMART goals, groups can confidently determine when real-time collaboration and collective work products are critical to their performance challenge. They can decide between the incremental, extra performance demanded of the team discipline versus the more expedient, sum of individual bests, characteristic of the single-leader discipline (see Figure 1.2 in Chapter 1).

Consider the following example. A branded clothing company has historically organized functionally around product, merchandising, sales, and sourcing. The CEO believes the company's poor performance arises from too few people with general management skills, so she decides to create five new strategic business units (SBUs). The five new general managers, the CEO, CFO, and head of Human Resources go offsite to discuss the new organization. Should this group apply the single-leader or the team discipline?

The activity-based aspiration, build general management skills, is no help in answering the question. Assume, then, the group works hard to answer the question, "How will we determine our success at building general management skills?" Among other things, they agree that general managers must become skilled at making trade-offs across different functions with the larger business in mind. The following two versions of a goal emerges from their deliberations:

1. *Version 1:* Each new general manager must deliver a budget within two months. The budgets must have at

least 20% year-over-year revenue, 10% profit growth, resulting in a return on invested capital of 16%. In addition, the plan must identify at least three major trade-offs, describe alternative rationales for making trade-off decisions, and defend the choice made in terms of each GM's own business.

2. *Version 2:* The five general managers working together with the CFO and head of HR must deliver a budget for the entire company in two months. This overall budget will encompass the budgets for each of the five separate SBUs. Both the overall and the separate business budgets must show year-over-year 20% revenue and 10% profit growth, resulting in an ROI of 16%. In addition, the group must identify key trade-offs, both within and across SBUs, as well as alternative rationales and choices made.

In Version 1, it is far more likely that the five new general managers can achieve the goal, as well as develop important new skills, through the sum of individual best performances. Remember, both the single-leader discipline and team discipline benefit from effective group behaviors, such as sharing best practices, constructive criticism, active listening, and positive reinforcement. Thus, the five people would gain from discussing and sharing what they were learning, although the degree to which they might do so would, in most organizations, undoubtedly suffer from the competition for resources and recognition among senior executives in charge of different businesses.

In Version 2, however, the group of seven people almost certainly needs to apply the team discipline. The identification of key trade-offs, as well as rationales for making choices are the kind of collective work products and incremental outcome that demands real-time integration of the multiple skills and perspectives within the group. For example, the budget for the whole business *must* be a collective work product. In this case, it is also likely that the overall budget will achieve more ambitious performance results because of the team potential that is invoked.

Please note: The senior executives at this company might responsibly choose either Version 1 or Version 2 as their goal. Each will advance their overall aspiration. Without the hard work of articulating these outcome-based goals, however, they really have no basis, other than instinct, for selecting between team and single-leader discipline. And, if they discuss teaming only in the context of their activity-based goal, of "building general management skills," they will fall into the trap of exclaiming to one another, "We have to really be a team to make this happen!"

EXERCISE 3.1
Outcomes Versus Activities

Ask your group to list the goals currently being pursued. If these are already written down, use the statements as described. If they are not in writing, then ask the group to articulate and write them down. Once you have a list of goal statements, discuss among yourselves whether and why you believe the goals are activity-based or outcome-based. For any you agree are activity-based, try to rewrite them as outcome-based.

EXERCISE 3.2
How Would You Know Success?

Gather your group and take fifteen to thirty minutes to review the challenges you face and how you are trying to meet them. Ask someone to keep a list of key objectives and phrases on a flip chart. Once you have finished this, ask yourselves the following critical questions: *How will you know you were successful? What will you measure, assess, or calibrate against?*

As you brainstorm and agree upon possible answers to this question, remember to avoid circular statements such as, "We would know we succeeded because we succeeded!" (e.g., "We will know we are communicating better when we are communicating better"). Also, be careful to recognize and acknowledge when your answers indicate activities, such as "We will succeed when we all understand the problem," versus outcomes, for example, "We will have succeeded when we have at least three new paying customers."

EXERCISE 3.3
Choose Your Yardsticks

Consider a performance challenge facing your group. Use Exercises 3.1 and 3.2 to help you begin to identify and articulate outcomes that would indicate success. Now brainstorm a list of metrics you might use to articulate your outcomes with greater specificity. Use the following columns to help:

Time/Speed	Cost	Defects/Errors	Positive Yields
_____	_____	_____	_____
_____	_____	_____	_____
_____	_____	_____	_____

Remember to think hard about both financial and non-financial metrics and try to identify leading and lagging indicators. When you have generated a good list, try to agree on one or more metrics that do the best job of reflecting success in a concurrent and direct manner. Then, try to articulate SMART, outcome-based goals using the selected metrics.

EXERCISE 3.4
Get SMART

Use the SMART criteria to construct outcome-based goals for your performance challenges. Use Table 3.1 to refine your goal statements.

TABLE 3.1 SMART criteria

	Yes, because:	No, because:
Specific?		
Measurable?		
Aggressive, yet achievable?		
Relevant to the challenge at hand?		
Time-bound?		

EXERCISE 3.5
Individual Versus Collective Work Products

Armed with SMART outcome-based goals, ask your group to discuss and decide whether success will require collective work products in addition to individual work products. Use Exercise 1.5 to help, only this time with your more specific goals in mind.

EXERCISE 3.6
Choose Your Disciplines

Ask your group to list the most pressing parts of the overall performance challenge at hand and convert each of those parts into one or more outcome-based goals. You might want to prioritize the top three, five, or seven goals. However you choose to approach your list, use the material in this chapter and Chapter 1 to discuss whether to use the team versus the single-leader discipline to accomplish each of the goals in front of you.

Note to Virtual Teams

Your group can do each of these exercises in a face-to-face meeting or with the help of groupware technology, such as threaded discussions, tele and videoconferencing, or chat-rooms. In our experience, if you are doing these exercises near the beginning of your effort, you will gain more from them in a face-to-face meeting because it will help members interpret, know, and develop respect for one another's skills and talents. Having said that, groups often face logistical and resource constraints that force them to debate and discuss the issues raised here through groupware, even toward the beginning of their efforts. If that is the case, please use the results of the exercises in Chapter 2 to guide your discussions. In particular, set rules and expectations regarding participation, time frames, use of questions whenever anyone fails to fully understand, and other particular requirements to be sure your dialogues are productive and that the absence of body language and other cues do not derail or mislead your discussions.

CHAPTER 4

Performance Agendas for Applying Both Disciplines

Striving for integration rather than compromise . . .

Many members of small groups in pursuit of increased performance capability tell us they are confronted with a wide variety of ongoing challenges *against which they must deploy themselves and others.* The groups cannot succeed without the flexibility and determination to deploy the single-leader and the team disciplines as needed to fit different performance tasks. The key, once again, is learning to balance the two disciplines within an integrated approach, not to sacrifice one for the other or compromise in ways that nullify full performance potential. By contrast, other groups have purposes, goals, and actions more concentrated on a single target and requiring effort only from the group members themselves. Unlike the more complex situation, these latter groups find it straightforward to choose between either the single-leader or team disciplines and pursue that choice rigorously.

Which of these two descriptions best characterizes the situation and challenge facing your group? In our experience, the following patterns often prevail:

1. Pattern 1:

   ■ If your group's challenge is near to frontline, operating work,

   ■ If impact is expected and required within a short time frame,

   ■ If the impact of your group's performance narrowly affects the entire organization's success,

   ■ If it is likely that members within your group will do all the work without assistance from others,

   Then

   ■ It is more likely your group can make a one-time choice between the two disciplines and move forward confidently until your performance challenge changes and requires choosing again.

2. Pattern 2:

   ■ If the effort of your group is further away from daily work,

   ■ If the time frame required to produce a significant performance impact is long,

   ■ If your group's performance impact has a broad and large effect on the entire organization's success,

   ■ If people beyond your group must participate and contribute,

   Then

   ■ It is more likely that your group must simultaneously and continuously integrate and rely on both the single-leader and team disciplines.

Pattern 1 often characterizes self-managing plant floor teams, sales teams, groups of customer service representatives in phone centers, and other functionally oriented and day-to-day operating groups who must produce similar results over reasonably short time frames ranging from an hour to a month or so. These groups must convert their purpose and challenge into one or more SMART outcome-based goals and consciously choose which of the two disciplines is most likely to produce success.

Teams assembled to recommend and implement changes with important but narrow impacts on the entire organization also fall in Pattern 1. For example, a cross-functional team seeking to reduce the time it takes to get promotion materials into the hands of salespeople might set a goal such as "cutting the time it takes to get salespeople new brochures from twenty-six weeks to eight weeks." This dramatic increase in performance will probably benefit from the team discipline approach. Once that is clear, the members can use the team discipline to meet their goal. A group pursuing a one-time, analytically driven challenge to "reduce the cost of issuing and sending accounts payable checks from four dollars to three dollars" is similarly situated, as is a group chartered with "developing recommendations for closing at least two new accounts over the next six weeks."

Groups finding themselves in Pattern 2 face more complex, longer-term, and broader performance challenges. Consider, for example, a team seeking to reengineer the entire process of sales generation through fulfillment. This team includes six executives from sales, marketing, operations, finance, customer service, and human resources. These six people will confront dozens of challenges well beyond getting brochures into salespeople's hands faster or doubling the number of new accounts in a sales region over the next six weeks. They should set an overall aspiration for accelerating the entire process. At the same time, they must improve revenue, profits, and customer satisfaction by a specified, significant amount. Such an overall SMART goal for their effort might be, "within four months, cut the cycle time of sales generation through fulfillment by two-thirds while generating 50% gains in revenues and profits and improving customer satisfaction at least 20%."

This ambitious reengineering target requires considering a wide range of required actions, both individual and group, many of which demand the articulation of sub-goals, as well as assigning responsibilities to individuals or sub-teams. Such critical to-dos include:

1. *Process mapping:* The reengineering team must get help to do both an "as is" and "should be" detailed diagram of all the activities and people involved in the entire sales generation through fulfillment process.

2. *Root cause analyses:* As the extended group (core team and helpers) considers the differences and critical gaps between what is and what should be, they need to determine the root causes. These are the fundamental determinants of things like cycle times, revenue generation, profitability, and customer satisfaction. A good root cause analysis is based on facts and figures, rather than opinions and anecdotes.

3. *Hypotheses and experiments:* The team must also conduct a variety of experimental efforts aimed at performance improvement. Given the seniority of the team members, most of these efforts involve people closer to the actual work of the sales generation through fulfillment process.

4. *Communications and involvement:* The team must find ways to keep all the affected employees and customers informed of progress and the implications of findings and actions. They will also need assistance from many of those same people throughout the reengineering effort.

5. *New organizational approaches:* No reengineering effort of this magnitude succeeds without significant shifts in both the formal and informal organization. Changes are required in formal elements, like job responsibilities, reporting relationships, information systems, compensation and reward approaches, and skill-sets. Changes are also required in informal elements like networks, relationships, ad hoc interactions, and flexible units. As the team works to identify and then implement such changes, a variety of sub-challenges will emerge.

6. *Implementation planning and delivery* that integrates with existing patterns and budgets: As the extended group carries out their implementation plans, the core team will want to limit disruption to others, employees as well as customers. They must strive to minimize any negative impact on shareholder results during the transition period. Again, this challenge produces a number of sub-challenges and sub-goals.

In this context, the six leaders will want to explore opportunities to apply both the team and single-leader disciplines, depending on the specific sub-goal and action at hand. They need to manage themselves and others to take full advantage of these flexible units because:

1. They cannot succeed by themselves; many other people have important contributions to make, sometimes as individuals and sometimes as sub-teams.

2. They cannot succeed if all six of members and outside contributors insist on participating in all aspects of the work; instead work must be allocated among the members and outside contributors in ways that are doable.

3. They cannot succeed if they assign themselves work strictly according to their own, respective functional expertise and hierarchical position. They need to use the team discipline to ensure cross-functional problem solving, creativity, and execution. And this cross-functional norm applies to others who get involved and make contributions.

4. They cannot succeed if they fail to take advantage of the functional experience, intrinsic talent, and skill represented in their group. They also need to use the single-leader or individual-accountability discipline when sub-goals and actions can best be achieved that way.

In addition, the reengineering team has to accomplish all of the above within realistic resource and time constraints. They operate within limits of time, money, people, and opportunity. They must plan, prioritize, and make wise resource trade-offs. Thus, conserving and growing the resources available to them is crucial, as is making the best use of those resources against tasks at hand. If an individual can accomplish a particular task, the team wastes time and resources by assigning it to a team. Conversely, if only a sub-team's multiple talents and skill-mix can succeed, the reengineering leaders squander resources and sacrifice performance by strictly adhering to individual accountability. Finally, if the reengineering team cannot prioritize in a credible way, the effort risks failure as people lose heart when they try to do everything at once because everything is top priority.

This reengineering team illustrates a common managerial challenge that confronts leadership teams with broad aspirations and responsibilities, be they teams at the very top or those who run single-business units, strategic alliances, joint ventures, shared services, major functions, or complex change initiatives. All such groups confront a complex, moving target of multiple challenges and goals. They cannot succeed by reducing the team versus single-leader choice to a once-only discussion or a personal favorite choice. They must break into sub-groups, involving others beyond the team, and capitalize on the diversity of the flexible units by choosing and applying both disciplines. The ultimate challenge is in learning to apply both disciplines as needed by each particular performance challenge and goal at hand. (For more on the unique challenges of leadership teams, see Jon Katzenbach's *Teams At The Top*.)

Performance Agendas for Leadership Teams

We have developed and successfully applied a simple management tool we call the *performance agenda*, designed to help small groups with multiple challenges gain clarity about goals and priorities. Properly used, this agenda enables any group to apply both disciplines as they manage themselves and others through the effort required by the challenges they face. Figure 4.1 presents the blank form of a performance agenda. Using it effectively requires the following steps:

Challenges we are resourcing	SMART outcome-based goals	Which discipline?	Responsibility (names)

Other challenges we face, but are not resourcing	Illustrative outcomes that would indicate success

FIGURE 4.1 Performance agenda for a small group

Articulate Your Team's Overall Aspiration

Assemble your team and devote the time needed to clarify and agree on the challenges you face, as well as the goals that will measure success (henceforth, our references to goals assume they meet the SMART conditions detailed in Chapter 3). Most teams confronted with broad challenges have experience articulating a vision, mission, charter, or purpose. That is what we mean by articulating your team's overall aspiration. Such statements are brief, convey a sense of urgency and importance, and usually identify a few themes that capture how the team's work will deliver value to customers, shareholders, employees, and others. More important, such statements are best when they are expressed in words that are simple, clear, and meaningful to each group member or participant in the effort. Katzenbach's book, *Real Change Leaders,* provides a number of illustrations of such statements that he describes as *working visions* because their simple messages work to capture the emotional commitment of those who both shape and pursue them.

Few teams, however, have much experience translating such statements into outcome-based goals. The Mindbook and Workbook sections of Chapters 1 and 3 will help such teams. In the above example, the reengineering team's original vision was to redesign the sales generation through fulfillment process to increase greatly the value delivered to customers and shareholders. The team converted this working vision into a goal statement that reads, "Within the next four months, cut the cycle time of sales generation through fulfillment by two-thirds while simultaneously generating 50% gains in revenues and profits and at least 20% improvement in customer satisfaction."

Break Aspirations into Sub-Challenges

Use brainstorming and other problem-solving techniques to answer the question, "What are the things we must do to accomplish our purpose and achieve our desired outcomes?"

The more complete the list, the better. A useful technique for compiling and categorizing such a list is called *clustering*. Give each person in your team a pad of adhesive-backed notes and, working singly or in pairs, spend the time needed to identify the specific tasks required to achieve your working vision and goals. Place the notes on a wall and let the group study and move all the notes into cohesive clusters of similar challenges and activities. This clustering effort rapidly eliminates redundancies, clarifies meanings, and generates a realistic list of what it will take to accomplish the overall aspiration and goals.

Identify What Contributions are Required from Others

Once you have produced a first-cut list of the key challenges and activities required for success, determine who else needs to get involved. If your group must lead a coordinated effort toward some aspiration with broad impact on the organization, its achievement is likely to warrant contributions from others. Potential contributors should be identified, whenever possible, by name and job type. Be sure to include people from supplier, partner, and customer organizations whenever they represent the skills best suited to the task. You want to end up with a specific list of who can best contribute to each key activity and challenge. At this point, however, do not concern yourselves with whether the people you identify have the time or permission to help.

Convert the List into Smart Goal(s)

Using the tools, techniques, and exercises in Chapters 1 and 3, a group can translate each major sub-challenge and activity into one or more outcome-based goals. In this way, team members and others can determine what work needs to be done, by whom, and toward what end. Such goals also put your team in a position to choose between the single-leader and the team discipline on a performance goal by performance goal basis. (See Chapter 3.) Finally, once the major sub-challenges are expressed as clear goals, a group can better assess whether the full impact of achieving those goals will produce the success required by the overall aspiration. If not, it's back to the drawing board to add goals or change aspirations. In other words, you need to determine whether and when it all adds up to the kind of total performance you want to accomplish.

Decide Which Challenges You Will Staff

Most groups approach this aspect of their effort through prioritization grounded in some notion of relative "importance." This approach can be a trap. While there are always gradations of importance among the various sub-challenges, many of the distinctions become difficult to make and are not that useful. Most of the sub-challenges a team identifies as essential are important to achieving its aspiration and goals. Thus, groups who pursue the "relative importance path" to prioritization often end up declaring their intention to do everything in ways that neither they nor others find credible. Having committed to prioritize, they actually end up not doing so. As a result, the expectations about who is responsible for what become completely unrealistic. Hence, they build in failure, not success.

Rather than launching into subjective and indeterminate debates about relative importance, we urge a review of your full list of challenges and aspirations and ask you to answer two questions:

1. First, will you assign responsibility and resources against the explicit goals associated with each sub-challenge and activity in question?

2. Second, will you demand and expect those assigned to devote the time and effort required for achievement of the outcome-based goal(s) within the expected time frames? In other words, *will specific people actually be identified, assigned, and held accountable* within specified time frames?

The first of these two questions is straightforward. Either you are able to assign resources, or you are not. The availability of the people you hope will make contributions is the most practical indicator of priority. A particular person or team who might be the best choice for help also might not be available. The group has the option of deferring the effort against the relevant sub-challenge until such resources become available. The second question is more difficult and demands candor. Do not mislead yourselves and others by bold-sounding but clearly unrealistic claims about what people are expected to contribute. Such bravado is an all too common mistake of ambitious groups; it wastes the time, energy, and scarce resources of everyone involved. It also destroys credibility and commitment.

Answering these two questions assists groups in setting priorities that reflect pragmatic realities about resources and capacity, rather than engaging in theoretical debates about relative importance. Regardless of how important any particular sub-challenge or activity may be to your overall aspiration, if you cannot resource the effort you will not achieve it. That is reality. If a group is unwilling to assign the necessary resources, for whatever reasons, or if the person(s) assigned cannot devote the time and effort to deliver against the goal(s), relative priorities are meaningless. In short, focus on what is doable, not what is theoretically desirable.

Finally, this step requires the group to decide how they will deploy themselves against the various sub-challenges and goals they identify. In other words, this step produces team member commitment. Most teams benefit from direct participation and contribution to the real work ahead. Members of the dreaded compromise units invariably position themselves solely as decision-makers and reviewers of the work of others. Do not make this mistake. Instead, figure out which of the sub-challenges and goals can best benefit from the personal effort of the people on your team, either individually or in combination with others, and hold yourselves accountable for those contributions and results.

Draw a Clear Line Between *Resourced* and *Not Resourced*

This simple line clearly separates what is being worked upon versus not worked upon. The line signals the group to concentrate on the challenges that we will call *above the line;* that is, those they will staff and set credible expectations for, versus those *below the line;* that is, those they cannot staff or set credible expectations for. But, challenges that go unresourced and are below the line are still important. Thus, false distinctions about relative importance are avoided. Teams can freely talk about all of the things required for their success without confusing themselves or others about what is currently being tackled versus what is being deferred. And, when sub-challenges and SMART outcomes that are above the line

are achieved, the team can address something important below the line by resourcing it and setting realistic expectations
regarding its accomplishment.

Choose the Best Discipline for Each Challenge Above the Line

For each sub-challenge and its related outcomes above the
line, decide whether the goals are more likely to be achieved
through the single-leader or the team discipline. Use what
you have learned in Chapters 1 and 3 to determine whether
the outcomes in question will benefit most from the sum of
individual work products and accountability with a context of
stable roles and single leadership. Or, decide whether they
demand an incremental, extra collective performance that
comes from the real-time application of team basics. Remember that this choice can be made either by the entire
group or by the specific people responsible for each sub-
challenge.

This step completes the initial performance agenda. If
your team has completed the initial template shown in Figure
4.1, you understand the working vision, what outcomes will
produce success at that vision, as well as the required detailed
set of sub-challenges and goals. You also have determined
which of those sub-challenges and goals will be currently resourced, above the line, and who is responsible for making
those contributions, both within and beyond your core team.
Most important, you will have decided which discipline is
best suited to achieve each of those contributions.

Monitor Performance and Make Adjustments

Use your performance agenda as the basis for reviewing
progress against the achievement of your vision and goals.
When individuals and/or teams succeed at various sub-

challenges, decide which of the additional challenges that are below the line should now get resourced. As new and unexpected demands appear, convert those into clear goals and choose whether to resource them and what people and which disciplines make most sense. As you and others succeed against the full list of challenges and goals, remember to recognize, celebrate, and communicate the sense of progress and accomplishment.

Preparing for Meetings and Work Sessions

The way a group prepares for and conducts meetings and work sessions makes a considerable difference to performance. Different approaches produce different behavior patterns and results. Unfortunately, most small groups and their leaders make the serious mistake of conducting all meetings in the same way. This leads to two different meeting patterns, neither of which is consistently productive.

The first pattern concentrates too much attention on the efficient use of time. Agendas, topics, and time frames are determined beforehand, and the leader tightly manages the session against those requirements. Many people prefer this approach because it minimizes meeting time, thereby conserving their personal time. The watchword of too many leaders seems to be that of "leveraging my time." When the primary purpose of the meeting is to share information, review progress, or syndicate decisions, a time-efficient meeting certainly makes sense. Such sessions, however, are not effective when groups must do real work together that goes beyond updates, approvals, and progress reviews. For example, if a group meets to make advances against a collective work product or to discuss and debate fundamental purposes, goals, or working approaches, the time-efficient agenda interferes with essential work. If all your meetings are leader-led, agenda-tight sessions, team levels of performance are highly unlikely.

The second pattern is worse. When there is no stated purpose or agenda for the meeting, discussions wander aimlessly in search of togetherness, communication, and empowerment. Decisions are seldom made, and end products rarely emerge, and, then, only by happenstance. Such sessions are completely undisciplined and frustrate all but those few members who use them to further personal agendas and dominate the discussion. Many committee meetings fall into this pattern, particularly when no clear performance purpose or goals are discussed or established.

The answer, of course, is to design meetings and work sessions to fit different tasks and performance imperatives. Simply put, you need different kinds of work sessions for different kinds of work products. As obvious as this may sound, few groups do this with any rigor or consistency. The following steps can help groups to design and conduct meetings that make the most sense for whatever job is at hand:

1. Define the purpose of the meeting in performance terms. Group sessions should rarely be held for the purpose of bonding or togetherness; those are byproducts of performance. Instead, such sessions should have a clear purpose that directly relates to the performance results required. Even the initial meeting of the group can have a performance purpose, that is, to clarify the charter, to gain commitment to a set of goals, to determine the working approach that will bring the right skill sets to bear at the right time, or to develop a performance agenda.

   If the purpose of the meeting requires real work by

the group, it is a good idea to ask some or all of the members to define that purpose, specifying the desired end products. On the other hand, if a meetings is needed to update each other, clarify individual work assignments, or provide leadership guidance, then schedule and efficiently run the meeting.

For any meeting or work session of the group, it is a good exercise for the leader or members responsible for the meeting to answer the following questions:

- What do we need to accomplish by the end of the meeting?

- Who needs to contribute to the set of accomplishments, and what kinds of contributions do we expect from various participants?

- What kinds of resistance or obstacles are we likely to encounter?

- How will we handle attempts to divert the meeting from its primary purpose?

- Who should lead the overall meeting, and who should lead the discussion/work on particular topics? Do we need to break into sub-groups for parts of the discussion? If so, what is the purpose of those sub-group sessions?

- Are we scheduling topics that are similar in their work requirements?

- Does the meeting require any special facilitation? If so, who should provide it?

- What kind of advance preparation is required, and who should be responsible for the preparation? Will the work be shared with all members prior to the meeting? If yes, will members be expected to contribute responses or otherwise demonstrate understanding?

2. Maintain a *two-bucket inventory* of issues and topics. Over the course of their efforts, small groups address many different kinds of issues and topics. It helps if both the leader and the members have established a consistent way of categorizing such issues and challenges to reflect time-efficiency needs versus open-ended, problem-solving needs. Groups benefit when the criteria for categorizing work in this way are clearly spelled out and understood by all. It is an important part of the discipline required for optimizing performance of the group. To that end, the following questions deserve the attention of the leader and/or the members:

   ■ Does this issue/topic require the skills of several members of the group, or does one individual know most of what is required to deal with it?

   ■ Can the required skills be applied best through each member working his/her part of the problem, or does it require two or more people working together?

   ■ If the issue/topic requires both individual and collective work, how important are the collective efforts?

   ■ What kind of skill/experience profile would best fit the collective work product portions of the issue/topic?

   ■ Do we need to be able to shift the leadership role during work session?

The first step toward addressing these questions is to plan a brainstorming session that produces a list of issues. It is helpful to limit the list to ten or twelve issues. If a large list emerges, however, you can employ any of several simple techniques to prioritize it. One easy approach is to give each member three different colored stick-on tabs, and allow them to apply the tabs to the list in order of their preference approach.

Once you have a list of reasonable size, ask the members to record and submit their answers to the above questions for each issue. Based upon the answers to the questions, the group should be able to categorize each issue. Members can also challenge particular categorizations as an issue that can be discussed in a time-efficient way versus a problem-solving, open-ended way. Ask one or two people to be *keepers of the buckets* as a way of forcing this categorization. The bucket-keepers play a valuable role in screening issue/topic candidates and can also maintain a rough prioritization of the topics within their bucket. At the end of the initial categorization exercise, you should have created a simple process whereby the bucket-keepers provide repositories for different kinds of issues as they emerge.

EXERCISE 4.1
How Complex is Your Challenge?

Gather your group to discuss the relative importance of simultaneously applying both the single-leader and team disciplines to your overall performance challenge. To do this, first spend time discussing and articulating the overall challenge ahead of you. Then, ask yourselves to assess the requirements and character of that challenge against the following criteria:

1. *Characteristics of work:* Closer or further from front-line, operating, day-to-day work? What is the relative proportion of the work time that will be spent on collective versus individual work products?

2. *Time to performance impact and completion:* Shorter term, completed within a day to several weeks, versus longer term, completed within several months to a year or longer? What is the time required to learn and apply team basics, and how does that compare with the time urgency of completing the task?

3. *Breadth of performance impact:* Narrower, performance outcomes represent a small impact on overall organization results, versus broader, performance impact represents major piece of overall organization results?

4. *Participation by others:* Only team members need to do work for success? Versus success will demand contributions from many people beyond your team?

5. *Stability of working approach:* Tasks are predictable and

recurring? Leadership role should be relatively constant and filled by a person who knows what is required?

Use your discussion of these questions to determine whether your small group's challenge is more like Pattern 1 or Pattern 2 reviewed early in this chapter.

EXERCISE 4.2
Articulating a Vision

If your discussions indicate that you are a leadership team whose success depends on significant contributions from other people beyond your team, use this exercise to shape and articulate a working vision, mission, or purpose statement for the overall challenge. Such a statement of purpose, or working vision, will meet the following criteria:

1. Capture the essence of the difference you are trying to bring about and why it is critical to the organization and those who will help you.

2. Emphasize no more than one to four basic themes.

3. Provide a rallying cry and basis for enthusiasm, as well as focus.

4. Be brief, memorable, and in words meaningful to all members of the group; avoid getting mired down in wordsmithing, but make the meanings clear. *out of weeds*

In our experience, groups are most successful when they move back and forth between (1) discussing the key themes, challenges, and performance differences they hope to make; and, (2) converting those discussions into phrases and statements. Groups can begin with either of these steps, go to the other, and then return to the first, and so on until the group is clear and coherent about what is the nature of its challenge; what kind of performance impacts it hopes to achieve; and how the language of its vision or purpose statement will convey the needed direction, themes, and inspiration to others.

EXERCISE 4.3
Convert Vision Into SMART Outcome-Based Goals

Once your group has a true working vision, or purpose statement, that meets the criteria in Exercise 4.2, work together to convert that vision into one or more overall clear goals that answer the question, "How will you know success?" You can use Exercises 3.2, 3.3, and 3.4 to help.

EXERCISE 4.4
Identifying Sub-Challenges and Developing a Plan

Gather your group for a half-day session to convert your vision and overall goals into a plan of action for success. Start by asking yourselves, "What are all the things we and/or others must do to accomplish our purpose and achieve our desired outcomes?" You should probably devote up to three-fourths of the half-day session to brainstorming, identifying, making sense of, and agreeing upon these key sub-challenges and activities.

You can use any number of brainstorming techniques to get started. We suggest using the clustering technique. Specifically, pair off, use adhesive-backed notes to identify as many sub-challenges and activities as possible, post those on a wall, and then spend time clustering similar ideas and themes. Other brainstorming techniques could also work. The key, however, is to avoid the trap of discussing possible sub-challenges as an entire team at the beginning. Such discussions inevitably reduce the number of possible ideas instead of expanding them.

Once you have put together a list of the major sub-challenge and activities, organize them into a coherent plan of action. The plan, at least at first blush, should meet the needs of your group's working vision and goals. The key question here is, "If our extended team were to successfully accomplish all the critical steps and actions indicated in this plan, would we be likely to achieve our vision and goals?"

EXERCISE 4.5
Create and Use Performance Agendas

Apply the following steps to create, and then use a performance agenda to manage the effort of your team and others:

1. Articulate your team's overall aspiration.

2. Break aspirations into sub-challenges.

3. Identify what will be required from others.

4. Convert the list into SMART goal(s).

5. Decide which challenges you will staff.

6. Draw a clear line between "resourced" and "not resourced."

7. Choose the right discipline for each challenge above the line.

8. Monitor performance, make adjustments.

EXERCISE 4.6
Preparing for Face-to-Face Meetings

Avoid the bad habit of running every meeting the same way. Instead, ask yourselves whether the purpose of the upcoming meeting is to update one another on progress and information, hear relevant, organization information from the group leader, discuss and resolve some logistical or administrative issues, and/or hear about decisions the group leader must make. If so, schedule a time-efficient meeting and respect everyone's time.

On the other hand, if the purpose of the meeting is to probe and explore ideas, and problem-solve, consider a more open-ended meeting. Also, consider thoughtful advance preparation to position topics and issues. Answer the following questions:

1. What do we need to accomplish by the end of the meeting?

2. Who needs to contribute to that set of accomplishments, and what kinds of contributions do we expect from various participants?

3. What kinds of resistance or obstacles are we likely to encounter?

4. How will we handle attempts to divert the meeting from its primary purpose?

5. Who should lead the overall meeting, and who should lead the discussion/work on particular topics? Do we need to break into sub-groups for parts of the discussion? If so, what is the purpose of those sub-group sessions?

6. Are we scheduling topics that are similar in their work requirements?

7. Does the meeting require any special facilitation? If so, who should provide it?

8. What kind of advance preparation is required, and who should be responsible for doing it? Will the work be shared with all members prior to the meeting? If yes, will members be expected to contribute responses or otherwise demonstrate understanding?

EXERCISE 4.7
Preparing for Virtual Meetings

If your group anticipates a virtual meeting, using a teleconference call or other groupware features, ask the same series of questions described in Exercise 4.6. However, be sure to tailor your answers and approaches to fit the differences between face-to-face sessions and virtual sessions. (See Chapters 2 and 8.) If the best approach to accomplishing the purpose of your meeting requires a time-efficient agenda, be sure to schedule the topics, updates, and discussions accordingly. Insofar as possible, ensure that everyone connected to the meeting is paying attention at all times.

Conversely, if the meeting has an open-ended, problem-solving purpose that will require the group to do real work, make sure that everyone is fully prepared and pay careful attention to how best to gain contributions. You might, for example, simultaneously use both the chatroom and teleconference features of groupware to carry on a virtual meeting.

CHAPTER 5

Applying the Team Discipline

Number and Skill

A small number—ideally less than 10 . . .

If there are more than ten to twelve people in your group, you may have too many people to apply the team discipline effectively. In our experience, the team discipline doesn't work with large numbers of people. We cannot claim that it is impossible for, say, fifteen, twenty-five, or even fifty people to operate as a real team—for short periods of time. We can, however, point to years of observation and scores of situations where large numbers were inconsistent with the discipline required for real-team performance. Large numbers favor single-leader and sub-team models or approaches; they do not require all members to do real work together to succeed. Moreover, large numbers cause the discipline to break down in ways that range from the obvious to the subtle, including:

1. Large groups cannot easily or frequently meet together. In the busy world of organizations, five to ten people are more likely to have the flexibility and control required

to get together as needed than twenty-five or fifty people. Even twelve to fifteen people find it difficult to schedule meetings they can all attend, much less engage in joint real-work efforts. While teams do not need to be constantly in meetings, they must spend time, particularly at the beginning and when they are stuck, working, learning, and shaping their mutual understanding of the challenge ahead. They need to agree on what they hope to accomplish and how they will proceed. For example, the group is too large to practice the team discipline if the people on the team: (1) do not have time in their calendars when they are all available, (2) cannot find meeting rooms that permit joint work, or (3) lack the travel and expense budget to pay for such sessions. While large groups who collaborate virtually across several locations and time zones have an easier time coordinating schedules, their meetings are not necessarily effective ones. Technology makes it easier to interact; it does not, however, make it easier to do the kind of open-ended, exploratory, and problem-solving work required for team performance. (See Chapters 2 and 8.)

2. Large groups are biased toward efficient meetings. The work of teams demands mutual exploration, open-ended work sessions, and commitment to use whatever time is needed to build common understanding. Team meetings, like all meetings, should have agendas that identify purpose and topics. But effective team meetings are rarely agenda-driven. They are issue-driven and must take whatever time is required to resolve the issues. Mindless pursuit of efficient time management invariably precludes effective issue resolution. When fifteen, twenty, or more people gather together, it is as

difficult to avoid agenda-driven meetings as it is to conduct issue-driven meetings.

3. Large groups are biased toward hierarchical leadership. Sheer numbers, plus the pressure associated with today's business world, drive large groups to want clear leadership. Teaming, by contrast, benefits from multiple leadership that shifts the lead role among the group on an as-needed basis. It takes time to build toward this kind of fluid team leadership. It also means working through frustrations related to ambiguity; something large groups rarely have the patience and persistence to do. Large groups are more comfortable with the hierarchical clarity that stems from a single leader and delegated direct reports who control group behaviors and working approach.

4. Large groups are biased toward stable roles. Greater numbers of members create greater pressure to assign and maintain clear, stable roles and contributions. Most often, these roles are based on job description, function, hierarchy, and position. Groups can achieve success this way when individual tasks and goals add up to the group's performance imperative. But if performance demands the flexibility and risk associated with the shifting roles and collective work products of the team discipline, people in large groups find it hard to sustain the required patience, experimentation, and personal risk taking.

5. Large groups usually fail to build common understanding and commitment. The common understanding and commitment characteristic of real teams arises directly from the members' mutual accountability for a compelling performance purpose. That kind of result re-

quires lots of discussion, interaction, and work. People on real teams can often complete one another's sentences. Members of large groups rarely reach this kind of shared understanding. Instead, we see members of large groups interrupting and competing with one another for airtime. They appear determined to protect each individual's functional and hierarchical position instead of blending those perspectives in service of performance.

6. Large groups often subdivide their challenges and work in ways that create smaller teams. This irony, and safety valve, for large groups is not always recognized. Their work must be frequently subdivided in ways that promote contributions from *subteams,* as well as individuals. The obstacles to teaming as a single, large group evaporate as the group splits up its goals, objectives, and work patterns. When this occurs, the subteams face few of the hurdles just described. They have the time, space, and budget to meet; they can have issue-driven instead of agenda-driven meetings; and they can develop the shared, fluid leadership, shifting roles, and mutual understanding and commitment required by the team discipline. Most important, the subgroups are in a position to apply either or both of the key disciplines that produce true performance units rather than effective groups. This difference can be significant.

If any of these difficulties mark your group's situation, then you may have trouble integrating the team discipline with the single-leader discipline. If so, you are unlikely to achieve a performance potential that exceeds *an effective group.* What should you do? We recommend the following three steps:

Step 1: Determine whether your group has performance challenges that demand the team discipline. Organizations often assemble large groups whose purposes do not require or benefit from teaming. For example, large task forces or oversight bodies and committees are asked to identify and decide critical issues. They may also serve as information-gathering and dissemination vehicles for decisions that range across such topics as corporate culture assessments, charitable activities, and community involvement. Often, such groupings are comprised of members with representative viewpoints who are appropriately concerned with different aspects of corporate governance. They might, for example, represent the views of different functions, levels, or other unit-by-unit divisions so that all relevant perspectives are considered.

These kinds of groupings, however, often do not face challenges that warrant either of the required two disciplines of true performance units. Their purpose is primarily to promote good communication and common understandings that help align individual efforts. If group performance is required, it is often easily met by applying the single-leader discipline, particularly in large groups. Thus, it is importan to ascertain whether your group will confront specific performance challenges that demand either of the performance unit disciplines, or whether effective group behavior is adequate. Moreover, if performance challenges warrant disciplined efforts beyond effective group fundamentals, the single-leader discipline approach works best in large groups.

Step 2: Determine who, among all potential contributors and members of the group, truly need to be committed to the team discipline for the specific challenge at hand. If you are in a large group that warrants the team discipline, you may still experience difficulties of size. In this case, it is critical to recognize that not everyone who is formally assigned to the effort needs to participate with those applying the team discipline. Many helpful roles do not require full, or real membership in the team. In particular three *contributory roles* assist the application of the team discipline:

1. *Sponsor.* Most organizations are familiar with the role of sponsor, an executive or group of executives who advocate in favor of meeting some particular challenge; commission a team; and, influence its resources, charter, and direction. Effective sponsors care about the success of the team; however, they are not working members. They oversee and support; they expect regular updates and communications. Sponsors also review and promote team efforts. But rarely do sponsors hold themselves mutually accountable for that team's success or roll up their sleeves and directly help with the real work of the team. In fact, the role of sponsor is hindered, if not nullified completely, when the sponsor functions as a working member or active leader of the team.

2. *Ad hoc contributor.* Teams often benefit from non-member contributors with something special to offer. Such individuals might provide a much-needed analysis, or access to critical expertise. They can educate the team about particular functional or technical matters, assist with facilitation and training, or support specific communications. Many such contributions provide relevant and helpful inputs to the team's efforts. Teams benefit the most when the ad hoc contributor under-

stands the team's purpose and goals and how his or her contribution can best help. But ad hoc contributors rarely need to develop the same level of commitment as full-fledged members of the team.

3. *Formal members.* The most subtle and difficult distinction in our experience is between a person who is formally designated a member of a group but not doing the real work or making the same level of commitment as other team members. This phenomenon deserves special attention. For example, departments, functions, or other units of the organization are often responsible for producing useful results that do not demand each and every person in the department or unit to contribute equally. At other times, as described above, different groupings are formed to include more people than required for team performance. There are even occasions when a small group, six to ten people, contains one or two members who simply will not commit to the basics. In this situation, the group or its sponsor may need to find ways for the noncommitted resources to contribute, that is, treat them as you would an ad hoc contributor. If this is not possible, and if their failure to commit blocks the team's performance, the only choice is for the sponsor or leader to replace them or otherwise nullify their disruptive influence. (See Chapter 9.)

Underlying the inclination to treat all people as part of the team is a dangerous assumption: If a person is present, then he or she must behave and be treated as a member of the team. Many well-meaning people are motivated toward this kind of inclusiveness. We don't like to offend people by suggesting "they are not on the team." Unfortunately, these natural human instincts cause people to confuse specialized role contributions with effective teaming and, as a consequence, get into trouble as team membership grows too large. Moreover, much valuable time is wasted trying to include them. Remember: Team is a discipline, not a limitless group of helpful people. All of the above distinctions reflect this difference. When people act as though sponsors, ad hoc contributors, and all formally designated individuals must be part of the team, they are thinking about team membership as if the team were an open-ended grouping within the organization, instead of a management discipline for achieving specific performance outcomes.

Certainly, you want to take advantage of the potential help of sponsors, ad hoc contributors, or other formally designated members of your group who can contribute to the team's goals in specialized ways. It is important, however, to candidly discuss roles and expectations. Keep them abreast of what the team is trying to accomplish, and make sure they know how their contribution fits the team purpose. But avoid allowing them to participate in every single aspect of committed member interactions. The real team must always be a small core of people with complementary skills, who are equally committed to a common purpose, common goals, and a commonly agreed upon working approach, to all of which team members will hold one another mutually accountable. There is no substitute for this discipline.

Step 3: Subdivide your overall challenge in ways that better accommodate the two disciplines that produce performance units.

If, after clarifying roles, your group is still too large to apply the team discipline, the most effective action is to subdivide the challenges into more manageable parts and consider both disciplines. The leader might do this alone or with the help of others. The objective is to identify and discuss the kind of performance challenges facing the group, the different outcomes to be achieved, the type of work that must get done, and the disciplines, single-leader or team, demanded by those goals and that work. Developing a *performance agenda* or using the *clustering* technique (both described in Chapter 4) can help with subdividing challenges and work into smaller pieces.

One additional device is called a *logic tree* illustrated in Table 5.1. (The term reflects the fact that when turned sideways, the diagram looks like a tree.) Logic trees break down larger problems and challenges into smaller ones. Start by briefly describing your group's challenge at the far left of the logic tree, that is, the tree trunk. What are the three to five most critical things that need to get done in order to succeed at this overall challenge? After you identify, discuss, and agree on these, write them down in the series of lines, or major branches, linked to the trunk. Next, what are the three to five most critical steps to accomplishing each of these major branches? Again, write them down. As your group works through this logic tree, a sensible pattern of sub-challenges and work ought to emerge. Once this happens, smaller groups can be assigned pieces of the overall challenge in ways that position them to apply the team discipline, or the single-leader discipline, as needed.

Complementary Skills

Can a team be too small? Only if it lacks the necessary talents, skills, or capacity to get the job done. Every successful team develops the required mix of skills and talent to deliver its performance objective. Nonetheless, we have yet to come

TABLE 5.1 Logic tree

Overall Challenge	Key Sub-Challenges	Critical Pieces of Sub-Challenges
		_____
		_____
	_____	_____
		_____
		_____
	_____	_____
		_____
		_____
		_____
_____	_____	_____
		_____
		_____
		_____
	_____	_____
		_____

across a team whose members had all the required skills at the beginning of their work together. Sometimes, the missing skills could be attributed to the small size of the group. More often, the gap had less to do with number than with the inevitable need for teams to grow and learn as they move forward.

This is hardly surprising. If a performance outcome can result from the sum of the contributions and work products of individual members working independently, then the team discipline is the wrong choice. The single-leader discipline will get the job done. The team discipline choice implies that individuals, acting alone, will not have all the answers, skills, experiences, and perspectives needed for success. It also often implies that these requirements do not exist within the total group at the outset. Therefore, in addition to a performance challenge, the group has a learning challenge. It follows that while the team might have the combination of skill and *skill potential* to get the job done, success will require learning and growth on the part of most members.

In forming a team, it is critical to consider skill potential and learning as much as existing skill. Naturally, leaders seek the best possible mix of people, talents, and skills. Unfortunately, however, too many team leaders fail to recognize that much of the team's learning will come after, not before, the team gets to work. As a consequence, they spend too much time searching for just the right people, instead of accepting people who have the potential to develop and learn the necessary skills. In doing so, they inadvertently lean toward the single-leader discipline.

Why? Leaders who focus exclusively on existing skills too often assign work based on existing skills. Unfortunately, this mind-set equates organizational role and functional skill with role and skill on the team. When the marketing person only does marketing, finance person only finance, and operations person only operations, the group is applying the single-leader discipline. Sometimes that approach will deliver the required performance results; sometimes it will not. If, however, the team discipline is needed, this emphasis on function creates a suboptimal constraint on team member roles even before team selection and work.

To avoid this trap, we recommend using the worksheet in Table 5.2 to help select team members. The worksheet asks leaders to assess candidates against specific skill, experience, and perspective requirements relevant to the performance challenge at hand. The worksheet is organized around the primary skill categories required for team performance: (1) functional and technical, (2) problem-solving and decision-making, and (3) interpersonal and teamwork.

Once a group has chosen to use the team discipline against any particular performance challenge, the members must convert *skill plus skill potential* into performance. Real teams learn to exploit the overlap in skills across the team so that people can assist one another when the need or occasion arises. Actions that build and transfer required skills in the team include:

1. Work assignments. The most potent learning vehicle available is work itself. By assigning work that taps into skill and skill potential, team members grow in ways needed for performance. For example, asking an engineer and finance manager to develop and conduct market surveys will provide each with a potent opportunity to learn new skills related to customer needs, marketing, and sales. Teams who take such risks accelerate their learning and advance more rapidly. Leaders of performance units that would accelerate their team capability are well advised to encourage those with skill and experience shortfalls to take on skill-building assignments. It is the wise leader who enables learning and

TABLE 5.2 Selecting the group

Describe your performance challenge: _____
_____
_____
_____
_____
Skill and skill potential needed:
Functional and technical: _____
_____
_____
_____
_____
Problem-solving and decision-making: _____
_____
_____
_____
Interpersonal/teamwork: _____
_____
_____
_____
What this person might contribute: _____
_____
_____
_____
What concerns/challenges/learning opportunities this person will face: _____
_____
_____
_____

skill enhancement even when it involves an occasional risk to performance.

2. Collective work products. Growth and learning rapidly accelerate when two or three people on the team work together on a collective work product. (See Chapter 1.) For example, consider a team in a biotech company that must design and implement a 360-degree feedback tool. The team concludes early on that this warrants the team discipline rather than a human resources manager working on it alone. The team hopes to discover what other biotech firms have done with 360-degree and similar approaches. If that assignment goes only to the human resources person, other team members will lose an opportunity to grow and learn in ways that are critical to success. More important, performance could suffer. The human resources manager, for example, might fail to observe or ask about certain aspects of how 360-degree worked in other companies that would more readily appear important to someone from IT, sales, marketing, or operations.

   The better approach is to ask the IT and marketing professionals to work together with the human resources manager to identify and interview other biotech firms as a collective work product. By including the human resources manager, the team has the chance to transfer some HR perspective and skill to the marketing and IT professionals and vice versa. Thus, collective work products provide opportunities for skill development and skill transfer that are relevant to performance.

3. Assessment of progress against performance goals. The best teams continually ask themselves what is working, what is not working, and what to do about it. They make

constant reference to their progress toward the team purpose and goals. Thus, every member enjoys a steep trip up the learning curve.

4. Ad hoc contributors. At times, teams need highly specialized or unique contributors. They have two basic choices in this case: (1) they can ask for the contribution, get it, and just move on; or (2) they can explore the options, learn and understand what various ad hoc contributors can offer, and choose accordingly. When it is critical for teams to incorporate new skills and perspectives, the latter choice is often the best. However, that choice implies assigning one or two team members the responsibility for coordinating with the ad hoc contributor in ways that accomplish both the performance and the learning objectives of the team. Imagine, for example, that the human resources manager in the biotech example was not a member of the team. By asking her to work as an ad hoc contributor with the IT and marketing team members, the same skill development and skill transfer objectives are achieved. A better collective work product is also likely to emerge.

Groupware technology expands the opportunities performance units have to receive ad hoc contributions from others within and even beyond their organizations. Chapter 8 describes why this is a double-edged sword. One edge of the sword offers increased access to ad hoc contributors, as well as accelerated cross-learning. The second edge comes from the risks associated with too many ad hoc contributors, as well as non-team members having too much opportunity to divert and confuse core team work.

5. Training and education. The most natural and obvious approach to learning or transferring skills is training

and education. Unfortunately, it is not always the best. Far too often training and education employs a passive, one-way context characterized by experts talking to or at teams in classroom formats. The focus is more on conveying the techniques, frameworks, and insights of the experts instead of applying whatever expertise is relevant to achieve the specific performance objectives and goals of the teams in attendance.

Even interactive case studies and Q&A sessions too often fail to concentrate on the real performance needs of those being trained. To deal with such obstacles, experts must be thoroughly briefed on the team's purpose and goals. They must also be prepared to demonstrate and teach how the new skills or expertise can be applied to the team's challenges versus "challenges in the abstract." Scheduling the training "just in time" is equally critical. "Just in time" is when the team is most in need of new ideas and approaches. Ideally, that is when it is actually encountering the kinds of obstacles or opportunities that the discussion and training can usefully address.

For example, quality and continuous improvement efforts should always include a "just-in-time" component. Instead of spending most or all of the training resources on a series of up-front, awareness-building sessions with attendance required by all, provide training only to teams who have already set specific, clear goals and who need help in achieving those goals. The sessions themselves are customized to concentrate only on those problem-solving and teaming techniques relevant to the goals at hand.

6. Personal feedback. Teams who seek to learn must figure out how best to get constructive feedback. Such feed-

back can come from those beyond the team, as well as giving and receiving feedback and evaluation to and from one another in the team. Even negative, personal feedback can be constructive if delivered in the proper context, namely how the improvement sought will advance the team toward achieving specific goals going forward. Obviously, the best teams take full advantage of positive feedback, especially positive feedback about a contribution or skill development that has moved the team closer to success. Time and again, we have observed that learning is cemented when a risk taken by anyone is followed with immediate and positive feedback along with expressions of appreciation by others on the team.

EXERCISE 5.1
Is Your Group Too Large to Apply the Team Discipline?

If your group has more than ten to twelve people, you should seriously consider breaking into subteams that could more easily apply the team discipline. Even if you have eight or less people in the group, you might want to take the self-test in Table 5.3 to determine whether size is a problem. If you find yourselves answering *Yes* more than *No*, your group is too large.

TABLE 5.3 Group test for discipline

	Yes	No
We spend more time trying to find a time when we can all meet than actually meeting.		
We never seem to have time in meetings to actually discuss anything.		
We have too many people and too little time to really understand each others' point of view.		
We'd be more efficient if the group leader would just tell each of us what to do.		
Our meetings would be too chaotic and frustrating if we didn't stick to the agenda.		
There is simply no way our entire group could ever meet more than once a month or so, even if we used conference calls. We're just too busy and have calendars that are too crowded.		

EXERCISE 5.2
Identifying Special Roles

If your group seems too large to apply the team discipline, try identifying the special contributors who do not need to attend all team meetings and discussions, but, instead, can be kept informed as needed. Such individuals might be sponsors, champions, ad hoc contributors, or advisors. Review the material at the beginning of this chapter and decide whether any of the people in your group fit this description. If so, how many? Are the remaining numbers now manageable? How can their role be rewarding even though the team chooses to regard them as a non-core contributor?

EXERCISE 5.3
Breaking Into Sub-Teams If Needed

If your group is too large to apply the team discipline, then you must break your overall challenge into subchallenges that can be assigned to individuals and subteams. You might do this by developing a performance agenda. (See Chapter 4.) Or, you might use the logic tree shown in Table 5.1.

EXERCISE 5.4
Picking People on Skill and Learning Potential

Use Table 5.2 to develop a profile of potential team members based on skill and skill potential. If you are a leader forming a group, you can do this on your own prior to naming the group. If a group has already been formed, then you might ask everyone in the group to participate. In this manner, the entire team will see where the strengths and gaps are between the skills and skill potential required by the performance challenge at hand versus those in the group.

EXERCISE 5.5
Identifying Relevant Skill Gaps

You can do this exercise in a meeting or through assignments to team members. Start with a good description of your performance challenge, key outcome-based goals, and the skills and experiences you believe are relevant to achieving them. You might also develop a performance agenda (see Chapter 4) as the basis for this exercise. Once you have defined what you believe are the relevant skills and experiences required for success, identify which of those you fear might be missing from your group. Obviously, this exercise demands constructive candor. The key here is to avoid personalizing anything. Instead, your purpose is to know what stands in the way of success for the entire group. One way to avoid that trap is to err on the side of making your list long, rather than short. In our experience, long lists of skill gaps often turn out to be more accurate than short lists and easier for the group to discuss in a nonpersonalized way.

EXERCISE 5.6
Strategies for Building Relevant Skills and Experiences

Using the list generated in Exercise 5.5, develop a series of specific strategies for building the relevant skills and experiences required. You can use Table 5.4 to help. Remember to include specific names of people who will lead each particular effort and to include their assignments as part of your performance agenda or work plan.

TABLE 5.4 Specific strategies for building skills

Skill/ Experience Gaps	Work Assignment	Collective Work Product	Ad Hoc Contributor	Training	Other
Customer Knowledge					
Total Quality					
Tools					
Etc.					
Etc.					
Etc.					
Etc.					
Etc.					

EXERCISE 5.7
Whole Group Feedback—What's Working and What's Not

You can use this exercise as the basis for an entire meeting, or you can learn to include it regularly as part of all team interactions. It is simple. With respect to your team's overall purpose as well as each specific SMART goal, ask yourselves three questions:

1. What is working well, and why?

2. What is not working well, and why?

3. What should we do differently to move forward, and why?

Make sure to capture the "lessons learned" from these discussions. And, remember to convert the implications for actions into part of your work plan.

CHAPTER 6

Applying the Team Discipline

Common Purpose, Goals, and Working Approach

Common versus consensus: integrating to get the best of opposing viewpoints

The most powerful force for effective teaming arises from a common performance purpose, common team goals, and a *commonly* agreed upon working approach. Common is not the same as consensus or complete agreement. The purpose is what drives the team; it is their vision and inspiration. SMART goals answer the question, "How will anyone know the team has succeeded?" The working approach is that combination of activities and tasks along with agreed upon attitudes and practices that help the team identify and perform the work needed for success. We have discussed SMART goals at length in Chapters 3 and 4. In this chapter, we will go more deeply into purpose and working approach. First, however, we discuss what we mean by *common*. We also point out why working to integrate the best of opposing views is superior to seeking consensus or settling for compromise.

Many teams fall short because they act as though purpose, goals, and working approach cannot be held in common without complete consensus among team members. Unfortunately, the word *consensus* has taken on an impractical meaning and set of requirements in most workplaces. As typically used, consensus means 100% agreement. All too often that leads to compromise solutions, which are invariably suboptimal. People feel that unless they all agree, they cannot move forward. Thus, if anyone on the team disagrees with any aspect of the team effort, the group becomes stymied. This assumption grinds teams down. They endlessly debate without resolving where they are headed or how to do their work. They persist until the objector(s) finally agrees to agree in name only. Because the organization won't wait forever, the consensus-dominated team invariably fails. Or, it reaches out for the single-leader, working-group discipline so the members *can just get on with it.* If the team discipline is truly required, of course, the team will fall short of success as it mindlessly pursues 100% agreement.

This all or nothing consensus approach gives each member veto power over the progress of the whole team. Most of us acknowledge the impracticality of this kind of all-inclusive consensus. Few of us really expect veto power over the teams we join. Rather, we anticipate the opportunity to be heard and respected, to influence the effort, to collaborate, and to achieve real progress against the mutual direction and goals that get set. Moreover, we become frustrated time and again when our group falls into the consensus trap. We perceive weakness in leadership or overly aggressive, self-centered, individual behavior by the perennial objectors. We soon get discouraged and develop a collective lack of enthusiasm for the job at hand. What we don't perceive or benefit from is a performance unit.

Those who pursue complete consensus, in effect, act as if disagreement is bad for a team. Nothing could be further from the reality of team performance. Constructive conflicts are a hallmark of great teams. Without disagreements, teams rarely generate the best, most creative solutions to the challenges at hand. They compromise rather than *integrate,* a term first and best defined in this context by Mary Parker Follett: Integration involves developing a solution that incorporates the best of two or more opposing views. There must be disagreement and constructive conflict that leads to enriched integration among opposing viewpoints. The challenge for teams is to learn from disagreement and find energy in constructive conflict; not get ruined by it.

Working to integrate the best of opposing views requires teams to learn that common and shared directions, clear goals, and disciplined working approaches do not require 100% intellectual and emotional agreement. Instead, a team shares its purpose, goals, and working approach if the people on the team meet two conditions: (1) demonstrable shared understanding that builds mutual respect, and (2) integrated dialogues that lead to better choices.

Shared Understanding Builds Mutual Respect

Ongoing disagreement does not preclude shared ideas or improved insight and understanding. If you and I are on a team whose challenge is to design and install a new personnel performance review system, we may disagree about the purpose, goals, and working approach of moving forward. For example, you might wish to emphasize results more than skills as the primary purpose of the new system. I might argue forcefully in favor of skill development. *Regardless of how often or effectively we debate our respective positions, we may continue throughout the life of the team to disagree with one another.* Assuming we both have credible rationales for our views, an integrated solution may emerge, that is, good ideas become better, the merit of ideas prevails, and appropriate skills come to the fore.

Our differences do not have to prevent a common and shared understanding. There are two categories of disagreement: enlightened and unenlightened. People with *enlightened disagreements* can demonstrate to each others' satisfaction, each others' point of view. They can articulate their foe's argument to their foe's complete satisfaction and, therefore, achieve shared and common understanding even in the absence of agreement. In fact, foes increase their mutual respect for one another. In this instance, if I can describe to your satisfaction why you believe in a results-orientation, then I demonstrably understand your point of view. And, if you can articulate my preference for stressing skills to my satisfaction, the reverse is also true. By contrast, people engaged in *unenlightened disagreements* cannot or will not demonstrate their full understanding of positions they oppose. Most important, fuller understanding on both sides of a debate will often lead to a better solution than either side would come to without the debate.

Choices Based on Integrating Dialogues

Disputants within the team have reached the point of enlightened disagreement when everyone can articulate to everyone elses' satisfaction the different points of view on any issue. The team must make a choice that ideally will reflect and integrate the best of the opposing views. Often, careful discussion shifts perspectives and can eliminate disagreement;

however, this need not occur for the team to move forward. Choices propel teams forward more than endless discussions. How teams make choices is part of the working approach we will discuss below. Teams might choose on the basis of a sense of the team, they might rely on the team leader to make choices, or they might vote. They might make choices in any number of ways. A choice on key issues, however, should always follow the pursuit of an integrated resolution, not a compromise. As long as there is demonstrable, shared understanding that builds mutual respect, everyone on the team should be confident that whatever choice is made is fully understood, even if not agreed upon, and reflects a sincere effort to integrate the best of opposing views by all team members.

Through building shared understanding, pursuing integration, and making choices, teams position themselves for performance. In the preceding example, if the team chooses to emphasize results more than skill development in the design of the new personnel performance review system, I may still disagree. But through my demonstrated understanding of why the team's choice makes sense, and my appreciation and respect for the teams effort to consider the best of my ideas, I am able to support the implementation of that choice. I can hold myself mutually accountable for the team's direction even if I continue to disagree. *Furthermore, if I hold back or give less than full effort, the rest of the team can see that my unsatisfactory contribution arises from a persistent lack of agreement rather than a lack of understanding.* In the discipline of teams, such nonsupport is unacceptable. By contrast, when teams demand 100% consensus, they set themselves up for an erosion of commitment because any person on the team can claim, "Well, I didn't really understand this choice."

Common Purpose

Common purpose provides the direction, meaning, and spirited energy that teams need to succeed. A clear sense of direction focuses the team on what to accomplish and how it fits within the organization's larger priorities. Meanings for each member emerge from the working to integrate the differing viewpoints that guide the team as it makes choices and works toward the achievement of its purpose. Tangible progress motivates the team toward success and helps team members put their collective, personal stamp on the work of the team. Teams without direction, meaning, and tangible progress are teams that flounder and disband.

Purpose shaping is not slogan making. While slogans, phrases, or logos might emerge to capture the direction and meaning driving the team, teams who confuse purposes with slogans miss the point. For example, consider two teams, both chartered to identify and spread *best practices of innovation* across their respective global companies. One, in a food products company, was asked by senior management to help worldwide divisions do a better job of moving new ideas from the laboratory to the consumer's kitchen. The other, in a consulting firm, was asked to speed up the syndication of effective consulting approaches from one office and practice to another.

Each team was labeled as a *best practices team*. But the similarity between the two teams ended there. To begin with, a far superior, more effective team purpose emerged in the food case than in the consulting case. The food company's best practices team believed its success was essential to the company's central strategic thrust of creating truly global brands. Moreover, it constantly promulgated that belief among its members, as well as others. If you walked into a team meeting, you felt the team's energy and pride. The fate of the entire company appeared to rely on this team's success because the team always spoke and acted that way. Yet, this company had never succeeded in transplanting a good idea across country borders unless the CEO and other top executives used brute, hierarchical power to ram acceptance down the throats and into the plans of country leaders. This team was determined to change that. This team's impossible dream was to reshape the future of its company.

A visit to a session of the best practices consulting team was very different. It felt more like going to the dentist or waiting in a very long line for your driver's license or passport. The team was unclear about why their effort mattered, and its members had no enthusiasm for figuring it out. They preferred to complain to one another about the strong, *not invented here,* aspects of their firm's culture. Most of the people on the team believed the firm's Managing Director and Executive Committee were the only ones who could change that. If the senior partners who had assembled the team wanted a list of best practices, the team would figure out some way to contact offices, request descriptions of best practices, and then collate and mail out such a list. But the team didn't really believe in itself or its purpose enough to make much of a difference. This team's common purpose was, in fact, "Let's get through this somehow and then go back to client work."

In each of these cases, senior management provided the initial team charter. This is typical. Rarely does a team arise entirely on its own. Nonetheless, the food industry best practices team owned its purpose, whereas the consulting team did not. Ownership is critical. Yet, ownership arises from spending time and working hard to craft a compelling team purpose, not from admonitions or grants of formal organizational authority. Even teams that operate within narrow and difficult constraints can and do shape compelling purposes that are owned by the team.

A front-line team at the *Tallahassee Democrat,* described in *The Wisdom of Teams,* was assigned a very narrow task of "eliminating advertising errors" in the newspaper. Before they emerged as a model high-performance team within the Knight-Ridder organization, the original narrow purpose had become to "improve customer service performance all across the newspaper." And the 14 front-line women who comprised that team most definitely owned the broader, as well as the narrower, purpose before management even realized it. This example demonstrates how ownership of effective purpose of a real team is a matter entirely within the hands of the team. Those who blame or point fingers at senior management for "not letting us own our purpose" mistake the reality of compelling purposes.

Team purpose and team goals work with one another like a two-cylinder engine. They reflect and reinforce one another. In the food industry case, the team specified clear goals concerning the number, speed, and commercial success of food product innovations spread across country borders. These goals became milestones on the team's path toward fulfilling the overarching purpose. Most teams receive this kind of broad direction from senior management and work hard to enrich that purpose, while also specifying common goals. Sometimes, however, senior management demands outcome-based goals, and the teams must build their sense of purpose by discovering the direction and meaning of what those goals are all about. Again, in our experience, it matters not whether teams work from purpose to goals, goals to purpose, or fluctuate back and forth. What does matter is that goals and purpose are held in common and reinforce each other in ways that make sense to each member.

Obviously, as teams get started, they must discuss purpose and goals. Figure 6.1 provides a series of questions that teams should answer in shaping their purpose and goals. Members need to approach these questions in the spirit of dialogue and discussion: Ultimately, common team purpose and goals must be owned by the team as a whole (where "common" is understood as shared understanding and integrated choice instead of one hundred percent consensus). Remember that it can take several team sessions, plus lots of work between meetings, before a compelling team purpose and set of goals emerges. Or, it might take a single meeting. Rare is the team that does not benefit by periodically devoting time to revisit, reaffirm, or even revise its original purpose and goals.

- What are we being asked to do? What should we be asked to do? How can any gaps between "are being asked" and "should be asked" be reconciled?

- Why does this work matter to each of us, our group, and our organization?

- How would we and others know we succeeded? (See Chapter 3 on goals.)

- What are the most critical themes and issues that emerge from discussing these questions?

- Why do we care about this work?

- How might we capture this discussion in a meaningful statement of purpose and goals?

- What kind of work will we need to do to achieve our purpose and goals?

FIGURE 6.1 The questions that shape team purpose

Following a best practice in software product development, teams usefully can adopt *version numbering schemes* to help capture and then improve on purpose and goals that evolve. For example, after an initial few sessions, the food industry best practices team expressed its purpose this way:

Version 1.0   Let's be the first group to really break ground with this challenge of global branding. Somehow, we've got to figure out ways to get people involved in sharing product innovations across borders.

Later, the team worked to refine their purpose and a second version emerged:

Version 2.0   We will use food product innovation to break down the barriers preventing our company from creating powerful, single global brands. At first, we hope, over the next three months, to help at least three pairs of country divisions on different continents to adopt and commercially exploit at least one food product innovation in a manner that demonstrably increases customer satisfaction, revenue, and profit.

Figure 6.2 provides the conditions that characterize effective team purposes.

- Fits/reinforces larger organizational purposes
- Fits/reinforces team performance goals
- Taps and inspires real enthusiasm and energy
- Is aggressive yet credible
- Is used by the team

FIGURE 6.2 Conditions of effective team purpose

Toward the beginning of a team's efforts, these elements should exist as a matter of logic and theory. Toward the end, they should reflect reality. In between, they sometimes require reshaping. Thus, in the food service example, the connection between spreading and speeding up innovations across borders logically aligned with the company's overarching strategic intent to build global brands. As this team did its work, and as more and more innovations moved across borders and into the marketplace, visible convergence occurred among the brand promises and related customer experiences on a country-by-country and product-by-product basis. Similarly, at the beginning, the initial goals of building at least three cross-country successes logically supported the thrust of the team's purpose. As these three goals were achieved and others emerged, the team saw a reality developing. The barriers to communications, common interest, sharing, and speed that had stymied any real syndication of best practices were breaking down.

Obviously, an effective team purpose is one that the team uses constantly to guide and motivate their efforts. The food services best practices team used their team purpose and goals to make a lasting and dramatic contribution to themselves and their company. The consulting best practices team did not. In fact, it took only a little time before members of the consulting team could not even remember their team purpose, a sure sign that nothing meaningful would happen.

Common Working Approach

A *working approach* is nothing more mysterious than the specifics of how a group intends to get the necessary work done. With the single-leader discipline, the working approach is spelled out by the leader: Individual roles and contributions are stable and fit people's job descriptions. The boss makes, monitors, and adjusts all key group decisions. The working approach in the team discipline is different: it is more ambiguous at the beginning and more flexible throughout.

A team's working approach should include the following elements:

1. Characteristics of the work itself. The team needs to decide how to divide up and reintegrate the technical, functional, process, and problem-solving tasks required for success: who on the team will work on what tasks, including the assignment of individual and collective work products. (See Chapter 1.)

2. Administration and logistics. Scheduling of meetings and vacation; preparing and submitting travel, budget, and expenses reports; arranging interviews and other meetings with outsiders. These are the kind of administrative and logistical tasks typically handled by the boss in the single-leader discipline, but shared in the team discipline.

3. Norms of behavior. An ethic of acceptable and unacceptable behavior inevitably arises within teams. Does everyone do equivalent amounts of work? If so, what constitutes "equivalent," in terms of time spent, products delivered, tasks undertaken, etc.? Which discussions and decisions are to be fact-based, and which are to be experience- or judgment-based? Is dialogue open and nonjudgmental? Do people listen well and offer constructive criticism? Will the team persistently seek out fresh perspectives, outside opinions, and new information? If so, how? How will the group maintain a strong orientation toward performance and results?

The manner in which these and similar questions get answered and followed often spells the difference between teams that succeed and those that don't.

4. Decision and choice making. In the single-leader discipline, the boss makes the key decisions. Not so in teams. Ultimately, the team as a whole must choose its path forward. To re-emphasize, teams must be disciplined about making informed and integrated choices. Still, teams must figure out a way to make critical decisions and choices that will have the full commitment and support of people on the team.

5. Evaluation of progress. The best teams continually ask themselves, "How are we doing?" They regularly review progress against their shared purpose and goals to discover what is working, what is not, and what they must do differently to succeed. Moreover, they are relentless in avoiding *denial syndromes*. To quote the famous sportscaster Howard Cosell, they "Tell it like it is."

6. Use of groupware technology. Any virtual team, or even a co-located team using groupware technology, must choose which features and applications are going to be utilized. They must also establish specific expectations and rules regarding their use as part of the team's working approach. Simply assuming that the technology aspects of the team's work will take care of themselves is a huge mistake. (See Chapters 2 and 8 for more discussion about the technology implications of an agreed upon working approach.)

Clearly this is a lot to cover. But remember that these issues are present in the single-leader discipline as well. It is just that they are well-understood and answered. In our experience, teams must grow into their working approach and their common levels of commitment to that approach. Rarely are all issues and questions about "how we will work together" resolved at the first meeting. Like much about teaming, developing a strong and adaptable working approach takes time.

Having said that, we strongly advocate the following best practices:

1. Think and act self-consciously in the first series of meetings and interactions. Be explicit and self-conscious about challenges, issues, and possible approaches, particularly in the early meetings of the team. In Chapters 1 through 4, we have repeatedly stressed that groups must make a conscious choice about when to apply the team discipline versus the single-leader discipline. We have emphasized that the group's performance purpose and goals ought to guide that choice. The more explicit groups are in their first series of meetings about the choices they face regarding purpose, goals, and disciplines, the more likely they are to get off to a good start. In addition, whenever groups choose to apply the team discipline, they must also carefully discuss the challenges and concerns they have regarding that discipline.

2. Hold purposeful and issue-driven meetings. Meetings ought to have clearly established purposes and be issue-driven. Teams should avoid a misplaced concern for time efficiency. If there are logistical, administrative, or other routine issues to resolve, a classic agenda-driven approach works. But teams always have critical issues that are not routine, and that demand dialogue, problem solving, brainstorming, and discussion. Such

issues deserve whatever time is required. Having said that, any group, whether applying the team or the single-leader discipline, benefits from a clear-stated purpose and set of objectives up front. (See Chapter 4 for more on preparing and choosing the best approach to meetings.)

3. Seek visible early wins. Without question, one of the more powerful ways to shape the working approach of a team is by identifying and achieving early wins; that is, narrow but meaningful short-term results that demonstrably move the team forward toward their goals. For example, early in their efforts the food services best practices team found a number of product innovations that could be transferred from one country to another without requiring any modification at all based on local tastes. Consequently, they were able to deliver results quickly and build momentum for themselves and their organization. In addition to pursuing such early wins, teams benefit by celebrating and learning from how and why they succeeded at them.

4. Establish a few clear expectations about and rules of behavior. We emphasize the word *few*. Over time, several behaviors will characterize the ethic of the team. But, in our experience, teams can err in spending too much time early on developing lengthy lists of promises they will make to one another as part of a broad social contract. Instead, we urge teams to identify a few key behaviors to emphasize from the beginning, such as showing up at meetings on time, focusing on performance, and everyone doing real work. Members should *immediately* apply and monitor their conformance to

these aspirations. Once a team has demonstrated the will to commit to and follow a few key behavioral norms, others are easier to add.

5. Early on, get into the habit of introducing outside perspectives and fresh facts. A trap for teams to avoid is that of becoming too focused on themselves and what they already know. The best teams never let this habit form. From the beginning, they seek out relevant viewpoints beyond the team (e.g., internal and external customers, senior executives, people in other functions or from key suppliers or partners). They also insist on fresh, new information and facts that are beyond the knowledge and experience of people in the team.

6. Build shared understanding, not consensus. From the beginning, avoid the trap of complete consensus. Convert all unenlightened disagreements into enlightened disagreements. Work to integrate the best of conflicting ideas; shun the very notions of consensus and compromise. Once disputant members can articulate each others' points of view, get on with it and make fully informed, integrated choices!

7. Pay close attention to language. As teams develop common levels of understanding about their purpose, goals, and working approach, key words and phrases emerge and take on special meaning. The language that will be meaningful to your team will differ in most ways from that of other teams. It will be your language and your meaning.

8. Find ways to provide constructively positive and negative feedback. The more quickly teams learn how to provide constructive, performance-based, and relevant feedback, both positive and negative, the quicker they

move beyond personality and feelings to real learning and performance. Somewhat paradoxically perhaps, the best feedback is actually focused forward on what lies ahead and how that relates to performance. Marshall Goldsmith recently coined the phrase *feedforward* to capture this emphasis.

EXERCISE 6.1
Build Shared Understanding through Enlightened Disagreements

Go ahead and disagree! In fact, welcome, encourage, and cel-ebrate disagreement. Differing points of view are a wellspring for team progress learning and performance. However, make sure you have enlightened disagreements. Be sure you strive to integrate rather than compromise the best of opposing views. Whenever a serious disagreement arises regarding any-thing essential to the progress of the team use this exercise: Once the disagreement is evident, identify the team members involved and label their positions in some convenient way (e.g., John supports position A versus Maria who supports po-sition B). If the disputants need facilitation, appoint someone on the team as referee. Let the debate continue until it begins to sound as though those involved are repeating themselves. That is a sure sign that it is time to ask each person to articu-late the opponent's point of view. In this case, for example, once John and Maria are repeating themselves in their argu-ment, ask John to articulate position B to Maria's satisfaction and Maria to articulate position A to John's satisfaction. Next, ask others to identify the best parts of both John and Maria's ideas. Then carefully consider if there are ways to get the best from both sets of ideas. For example, is there a third option that integrates some of both?

This exercise is similar to formal debating in that people are asked to defend a point of view different from their own. Most adults can do this, but it takes work. Again, in this case, ask everyone else on the team to critique how John and Mary do in defending their opponents' point of view. Be explicit about what is best about each opposing point of view. Also, ask John and Mary to objectively and fairly criticize each other. If either fails to do a satisfactory job, find out why and repeat the exercise. Once each party can truly articulate the opposite point of view to everyone's satisfaction, the team is ready to make a choice and move on.

EXERCISE 6.2
Purposing

Use the questions in Figure 6.1 to hold a purposing discussion. If there are disagreements, apply Exercise 6.1 to ensure shared understanding. This discussion may take two or three hours. It will work best if you meet face-to-face, but, if you must use technology, then use the lessons from Chapters 2 and 8, as well as Exercise 4.7 to prepare.

As your group discusses each of the questions in Figure 6.1, ask one or two members to make notes of the major themes that emerge, or, consider the clustering technique reviewed in Chapter 4. But, do not make the mistake of just talking about issues without learning from your discussion by summarizing conclusions, alternatives, tradeoffs, and possible actions.

Once you have moved through the agenda of questions in Figure 6.1 and captured the main themes of what your group sees as its purpose and challenge, move on to Exercise 6.3.

EXERCISE 6.3
Purpose/Vision Statement

Once your team has thoroughly considered and raised the major aspects of your challenge and discussed why it is important (see Exercise 6.2), write down a brief purpose or vision statement that captures the essence of what your team is attempting. Try to avoid excessive wordsmithing or nit-picking as you strive for concise, common meanings that tap the emotional commitment of each member. Usually, the meanings emerge first, and the exact wording comes along later. You might do this as a whole group, or you might ask people to pair off and spend five to ten minutes formulating purpose statements and then sharing their suggestions with the full group. As you shape, discuss, and choose among a variety of suggestions, use the criteria in Figure 6.2 as a guide to effective team purpose statements.

EXERCISE 6.4
Common Goals and Early Wins

Use your team's purpose statement to shape outcome-based goals that answer the question, "How will you know you succeeded at your team's purpose?" Refer to Chapters 1, 3, and 4, plus relevant exercises. Once you have developed a list of SMART outcome-based goals that make sense to your team, ask yourselves which of them can be accomplished relatively quickly? Revisit your team's purpose and goals as necessary until you are able to identify a few short-term goals that will give the team an early sense of progress, accomplishment, and momentum. Once you identify a few such early wins, assign appropriate responsibility within the team for their accomplishment.

EXERCISE 6.5
Working Approach

Spend time agreeing upon a basic working approach for your team. In particular, make sure you identify two or three rules of behavior that everyone on the team believes are critical to successful team performance. Avoid trying to set rules on everything; if your team gets beyond three or four rules, be careful: a long list is worse than no list at all. In addition, make sure you discuss logistics and basic administration. Look for opportunities to share the logistical and administrative load among all members. For example, perhaps you could take turns arranging meetings. Discuss workload and assignments as they relate and derive from the team purpose and goals. Use the performance agenda described in Chapter 4 to divide up work assignments. Finally, to the extent that your team will use technology, follow the suggestions of Chapters 2 and 8 to ensure you have agreed among yourselves which groupware features you will use and what mutual expectations you have regarding their use in virtual team situations.

EXERCISE 6.6
Words, Words, Words

Use this exercise whenever your team is ready to identify key words, phrases, and meanings that clarify what you are trying to accomplish versus *not* trying to accomplish. All team efforts discover such words and meanings. Often, they arise from within the team itself. Other times, people beyond the team respond to words and phrases in meaningful and powerful ways. Whenever anyone on the team believes a key word or phrase has been coined, spend the time you need to discuss why that word or phrase is so critical to your team purpose and goals, what you mean by that word or phrase versus what you do *not* mean. Also, decide how you wish to move forward in using that word or phrase as central part of your communications beyond the team. Remember, team performance is mostly about discipline, so if you are undisciplined in your use of team language, you are likely to be undisciplined in your behaviors.

EXERCISE 6.7
What's Working and What's Not

On a regular basis, use Exercise 5.7 with regard to team purpose, goals, and working approach to ensure your team is progressing toward performance.

CHAPTER 7

Applying the Team Discipline

Mutual and Individual Accountability

I want to know who is accountable!!

How many times have we heard an admonishment for the sound management principle of clear accountability? No self-respecting supervisory, managerial, or executive leader would argue against it. Nor would any member of a small group underrate the importance of being accountable for individual contributions to the group's results. This is more than a fundamental precept of consequence management: it is common sense.

The problem is that many of today's most critical performance challenges cannot be accomplished through the sum of individual best efforts and skills. Instead, collective work products are needed.

Collective work products demand important work contributions that have three attributes: (1) two or more people with multiple skills working together, (2) leadership roles that shift, and (3) joint, or mutual, accountability for results that cannot be obtained without more than one person being held responsible. A collective work product also requires some measure of individual accountability. Again, we see the wisdom and relevance of a *both/and* point of view, instead of an *either/or* point of view. (See *Taking Charge of Change* by Doug Smith.) Both individual accountability and mutual accountability produce team performance. Conversely, acting as though you must have either individual accountability or mutual accountability prevents team performance. While one of the core litmus tests of a real team is its sense of mutual accountability, team performance does not occur without each member taking on individual responsibility for many tasks, including the contribution of their skill to collective work products. A team effort depends on both, whereas a leader-led effort can mostly rely on individual work products.

Resistance to Integration

As obvious as the integration of mutual and individual accountability may seem, many leaders find it difficult to blend them. They are more comfortable with consequence management grounded in individual accountability. Most managerial experiences, habits, and practices more easily relate to holding someone responsible for doing their job, delivering an end product, and meeting a deadline. In this way, we make sure that one person has the responsibility for every single outcome of value, provided, of course, we can anticipate every single outcome. Classic hierarchy itself is an attempt to create discrete lines and boxes that clearly pinpoint individual responsibility and division of labor. In fact, advancement in any organization goes to individuals, not groups or teams. If you want to get ahead in your organization, the best way is to be sure that your individual accomplishments are recognized by the boss. If everyone in an organization could only know who and what belongs in every box, life would be a lot simpler.

Conversely, by resisting the integration of mutual and individual accountability, we avoid the apparent "fuzziness" of mutual accountability, i.e., when no one person is clearly accountable and, therefore, everyone is "off the hook" if things don't work out. There is no question that individual accountability is a more comfortable notion for the control-minded leader. Leaders want to put the "monkey on someone else's back," since it creates constructive anxiety, clarity, and pressure for getting results. Having one person to look to for getting the job done is a lot cleaner than relying on a group. And, there is little doubt that it takes more discipline and hard work to ensure that mutual accountability does not, in fact, let everyone off the hook. Like most things that are worthwhile, however, the extra work required to integrate individual with mutual accountability really pays off when it comes to team performance challenges.

Building a Sense of Mutual Accountability

Building a sense of mutual accountability within a group that already has a compelling performance purpose is far easier in practice than most people believe. In fact, gaining commitment to a common purpose and a set of clear goals is half the battle. At the same time, mutual accountability requires more than bonding exercises and mutual expressions of support within the group. Feeling good about one another is not the same as holding one another mutually accountable for specific and demanding outcomes.

Implicit in a sense of mutual accountability is careful attention to language, as well as metrics and outcomes. Again, the U.S. Marines provide a powerful example of the importance of language in building individual and the team discipline. From the first moment USMC recruits set foot on Parris Island, they are prohibited from referring to themselves in the first person. For twelve weeks, they must use the term *this recruit* in all personal references, rather than the more natural *I* or *me*. The explanation given to any outsider about this rather odd rule is simply *there is no I in team*. Of course, the language rules for recruits extends beyond the I-rule and reflects the USMC's unique insight into the importance of language in influencing behaviors. With respect to teams, if you are undisciplined in language, you are likely to be undisciplined in ensuring the behavior that team performance demands. Small groups with team performance opportunities must develop a common language around the key elements of team basics. Careless language promotes careless and undisciplined behavior.

Of course, language alone will not produce mutual accountability. Just like individual accountability, the concept requires clarity regarding performance outcomes, along with clarity regarding metrics used to track progress and the milestones used to determine pace. People cannot hold themselves accountable for collective performance unless they agree on goals and time frames. As simple as this sounds, it is too easy for a small group to harbor different views about outcomes, measures, and schedules. Small groups should be rigorous about goals, measures, and deadlines, and they must do so on a firm foundation of demonstrable, shared understanding. (See Chapter 6.)

Recognition and reward are also an integral part of mutual accountability. But, most recognition and reward systems are individually conceived and implemented. Compensation systems are designed to reward individuals, and gainsharing programs are designed to reward large groups. Small-group achievements seldom fit into these programs. Hence, it falls upon the group itself, occasionally assisted by wise and perceptive sponsors, to recognize and celebrate team accomplishments. The more a group pays attention to joint achievements, the stronger the sense of mutual accountability. In particular, recognizing the completion of collective work products and goals is at the heart of what mutual accountability is all about. "We are all in this together. We hold ourselves jointly accountable for our achievements."

How your group handles failures and setbacks is also relevant to building a sense of mutual accountability. In a real team effort, based on mutual respect among all members, individuals do not fail; only the team can fail. Pointing the finger of blame at one person invariably diminishes mutual accountability and promotes devisiveness. As a result, fingerpointing is a rare occurrence among real teammates. This is not to say that members do not have important individual responsibilities and tasks for which they are accountable to the group. Nor does it mean an absence of constructive feedback to one another. What it does say, however, is that for those important collective work products that determine team levels of performance, blame, and credit are a collective, not individual, matter. Needless to say, of course, any member of the team who consistently falls short of group expectations and performance requirements will invariably be excluded from key work product assignments. If the shortfalls continue, that person will be dropped or otherwise excluded from the team.

What Not To Do

If your group aspires to team performance there are a number of things to avoid because they seriously erode the sense of mutual accountability.

1. Do not perpetuate inflexible roles. In a group performance situation, there is a strong temptation to want to create clear, stable roles for each of the members. In some cases, this makes sense, especially where each member brings a special set of skills and experience to the group that can be best captured in a clearly defined role that exploits those skills. Certainly, a real team benefits from a membership that is comprised of complementary skill-sets deployed in ways that fit the group's performance purpose. However, a powerful advantage of being a team is the capacity to use different talents and skill-sets in multiple ways that are seldom best-defined by permanent or inflexible roles. For members to capitalize on role shifts, it is essential for them to have a sense of mutual accountability that causes the group to seek out creative ways to use their innate talents and acquired skills in multiple roles without eroding the performance discipline.

2. Do not allow *share of voice* to become a function of hierarchy. If dialogue and problem-solving exchanges are dominated by those at the top of the formal hierarchy, the opportunity for each member to contribute in different ways is severely hampered. Teams invariably find ways to open discussions to every member and ensure that equivalent weight is accorded to everyone's point of view, regardless of seniority, title, job, or function. The merit, rather than the source of the idea, is what should determine the attention it receives. Moreover,

the more ideas that are encouraged, the richer the knowledge base of the group becomes; any hierarchical filtering of ideas reduces that base. It also reduces the members' sense of mutual accountability because it suggests that seniority and position are controlling the output of the group.

3. Do not assign work based on job title. Working skills are much more important than formal titles in achieving team levels of performance. Members of the group immediately recognize when assignments are determined by job title or position in the hierarchy, and they will feel little accountability for one anothers' efforts if they believe tasks are assigned suboptimally relative to working skills and intrinsic talents. Another, even more discouraging pattern is when the grunt work of the team is always delegated to the junior members, with senior members as overseers or in advisory roles. When the higher titled members never get their hands dirty, team performance suffers. Mutual accountability requires members to believe that work assignments go the people best able to deliver results and that everyone on the team does equivalent amounts of real work.

4. Do not create special member immunities. No member of the group, including the formal leader, should be immune from the real work of the team. Nor should any member be immune from the more difficult or mundane tasks or agreed upon norms of behavior. Members feel mutual accountability only when they believe that each person is equally sharing the unskilled or tedious tasks. The reverse is also true: no member should be immune from leading the group when the task warrants it. In fact, the work assignments should be made in ways

that help each member develop new skills and attain higher levels of existing skills. As the members see their personal growth become a reality, feelings of confidence, commitment, and mutual accountability strengthen.

5. Do not look to the leader to make all key decisions. It is not surprising that many group members like to avoid the burden of decision-making, particularly on controversial or difficult decisions. The nondecision-making role is the more comfortable position to be in; groups that fall into this pattern, however, are missing three very powerful factors that contribute to strong mutual accountability: (1) the opportunity to optimize the leadership capability within the group, (2) the opportunity for all members to build their own decision-making confidence, and (3) the sense of accountability for the decisions made.

6. Do not allow strong personalities to dominate. Every group has two or three people whose style and personality lead them to dominate discussions, dialogues, and decisions. Left to their natural instincts, these members will take over the group process while the less outgoing personalities tend to allow that to happen. Again, this kind of imbalance can result in a loss of ideas, experience, judgment, and overall leadership capacity. It often requires conscious action either by the group, the team leader, or sponsoring authority to counter this tendency by the way in which agendas are constructed, assignments developed, and interactions encouraged. The purpose here is to integrate the best that both dominant and shy people offer, not to exclude the input of either.

7. Do not permit shy members to hang back. Equally unfortunate is the group whose shy members remain quietly in the background. Many potentially significant contributors are not comfortable stepping out in front of a group. Some would rather work on their own, let others influence and decide, and respond rather than initiate in a group setting. Such members, however, represent hidden potential that the team process is intended to uncover. The beauty of a well-functioning real team is the capacity of the group to stimulate, encourage, and motivate reticent members to seize the initiative and contribute in ways that exceed their own expectations, not to mention the expectations of others.

8. Do not fail to discipline disruptive or noncontributing members. Too often, well-intended groups who aspire to perform as a team are reluctant to discipline members whose actions are counterproductive. They assume that tough, no-nonsense prohibitions on disruptions or punitive actions against persistent non-contributors are somehow inconsistent with teaming. In fact, some of our descriptions of mutual accountability can be interpreted in that way. However, the basic notion of mutual accountability requires that the group must discipline its own nonperformers, as well as recognize, enable, and encourage the better performers. Mutual accountability does not mean covering up for the disrupters and noncontributors; it means dealing with them in a way that yields the desired performance result. Sometimes that requires replacing team members, sometimes it requires punishing them, and sometimes it requires working with them. The real team does whatever it takes to eliminate disruptive behavior

and ensure productive contributions from all of its members.

The above list of what not-to-do is important. In fact, this list is as important as the establishment of clear goals, metrics, and milestones. Goals, metrics, and milestones are only the first step in ensuring mutual accountability; elimination of these accountability killers is also imperative.

How to Know If You're Mutually Accountable

So what exactly does mutual accountability look and feel like? How can a group sense the level of mutual accountability among its members? Unfortunately, there is no magical screening mechanism that lights up when mutual accountability is working. There are, however, a number of questions to ask and conditions to look for that signify that mutual accountability is *alive and well.* Conversely, there are a number of red flags to watch for that signify weak or nonexistent mutual accountability. Let's first look at some of the best indicators of alive and well.

Alive-and-Well Indicators

The first place to look, or listen, is in the team's language. Whenever a group's actions and results reflect a strong sense of mutual accountability, members invariably use *we* or *our,* in reference to the group's goals, tasks, and targets. As described earlier, new USMC recruits are not allowed to use the terms *I* or *me* at any time during their entire twelve weeks of boot camp. Perhaps the USMC is the extreme, but, the trade-off *me* or *you* is seldom used when members of a real team are talking about their purpose, goals, and working approach.

Reflecting this same attitude, we observe a notable absence of finger-pointing in the group's interactions. Even when groups get stuck and frustrations and pressures become intense, team members seldom single one another out for blame; instead they focus forward on what needs to be done collectively "by us." Rather than fixate on who did what wrong, they talk about how multiple members can step up the pace or take up the slack by working *together* in different ways. At the same time, this emphasis on collective terminology does not prevent them from bringing pressure to bear on dysfunctional members. While it is true that no one person can fail in a real team, it is also true that no one person is allowed to cause the team to fail.

Common metrics or indicators of success are another important indicator. Each member has a common view of success, and how the group's accomplishments will be measured or determined. Not every desired outcome will be numerically measurable, but each should have clearly recognizable conditions of achievement. Each member of the group will describe those conditions in the same way, often using the same words. In the case of the Sony Dream Team that penetrated 20% of the Japanese market for engineering work stations in record time, success was described in product characteristics. In the case of the Tallahassee Democrat's Elite Team, success evolved from "eliminating advertising errors" to "creating a new level of customer service." Different metrics, each of which were clearly articulated by every member of these high-performing teams. If the members of your team cannot articulate the indicators of success in agreed-upon terms, mutual accountability is unlikely to be alive and well.

A final important indicator of mutual accountability is the relative weight, number, and clarity of collective work products versus individual work products. Do all members of the team recognize the difference between the outcomes or products that must be delivered jointly versus those that can be delivered individually? And are those joint deliverables of high priority and of greater importance to the team's mission or overall purpose than those that are deliverable by individual members working on their own? The relative importance of collective work products is a critical litmus test for choosing the appropriate discipline; it is also an excellent indicator of the need for and the existence of mutual accountability.

Red Flags

The following six items are red flags, or early warning signs, of trouble:

1. Most work assignments go to individuals singly. It is normal and natural to want to put someone's name beside each task, goal, and outcome. In that way, the group can ensure that the job will be completed, and the leader can know who is responsible for what. This is the heart of individual consequence management and is second nature to most good managers. Unfortunately, it precludes mutual accountability. Unless important tasks and outcomes require multiple names, you will not deliver the collective work products that are critical to team levels of performance.

2. One-on-one discussions dominate meetings. Good managers like to talk directly to the person responsible for a task. That attitude will produce meetings in which each member of the team has a specified topic and time to report, and any issues will be discussed largely between that topic leader and the formal group leader. Hence, for most of the time in most meetings, most of the members are but an audience asking occasional questions. They are neither active participants nor

responsible problem solvers or contributors. Mutual accountability fades quickly in this kind of meeting.

3. The group's only metrics are budget-like financial numbers. The group is defined by its budget. Outcomes are expressed in either increased revenues or reduced costs, and resources are prescribed by numerical calculus (headcount × compensation × time). Every task of the group can easily be translated into financial numbers. Again, this signifies the kind of consequence management that precludes mutual accountability. It lacks the flexibility for the group to determine how it wants to hold itself accountable, and what will constitute meaningful indicators of success including nonfinancial outcomes. Strictly by-the-numbers accountability also lacks motivational content.

4. All meetings adhere to tight agendas and schedules. We all abhor meetings that wander aimlessly from topic to topic, reaching no actionable conclusions and wasting valuable time on side issues. To avoid such agonies, well-meaning leaders strive for clear agendas and predetermined time frames. A good meeting is often defined as one that begins on time, ends on time, and covers all the topics on the agenda. Unfortunately, such meetings allow no time for the kind of open dialogue, joint problem solving, and group design work that real team performance requires. As a result, there is no need or opportunity for mutual accountability to prevail.

5. The formal leader does little real work. Good leaders are good at delegating. They are also masters of leveraging their own time, sometimes at the expense of others' time. Some say that the best leader will have little to do

because of the ability to delegate the real work to others. In a single leader-led group, this attitude is appropriate and effective; in a team, it is corrosive. Team leaders must be resourceful gap-fillers. They need to always be on the alert for work that isn't being done effectively and quick to step into the breach to make things happen. In that role, team leaders are the catalysts for mutual accountability because they shoulder some of the load, rather than exclusively directing others to do all the work.

6. The group has added nothing to the charter supplied by the sponsor. If a group exerts no influence on outcomes, the members will feel little or no mutual accountability. Rather, they quickly gravitate to clarifying their individual roles or work assignments and getting that job done. If the group believes time spent *purposing,* or reshaping, group goals and metrics is time wasted, because the sponsor has prescribed the results, no mutual accountability will emerge.

Much of the challenge in integrating mutual and individual accountability comes from being clear about what the mutual and individual goals or outcomes and tasks really are. Hence, the exercises that we suggest for establishing mutual accountability and keeping it alive and well have to do with sorting out the tasks and metrics. Nonetheless, since the natural mind-set in most well-run enterprises favors individual accountability, the following six exercises are worth the effort.

EXERCISE 7.1
Identifying Collective Work Products Versus Individual Work Products

Determine the relative importance and urgency of collective work products relative to the group's mission and purpose. Exercise 3.5 is an excellent starting point. Categorize expected outcomes or work products as either collectively or individually delivered. Then you can readily assess the relative importance of the contents of each to the achievement of the overall group purpose and definition of success.

EXERCISE 7.2
Recasting Collective Work Products as Individual Work Products, and Vice Versa

Identify three collective work products and change the conditions so that they become individual work products, and vice versa. Note the trade-offs. This exercise usually works best when two breakout groups work separately, but simultaneously, on the same sets of products. However, one of the groups is instructed to craft a set of conditions that favor individual products, while the second group focuses its attention on shaping collective products and outcomes. Then, the two groups reverse roles so that both groups have a chance at shaping individual, as well as collective outcomes. Finally, the breakout groups reconvene and discuss their conclusions in an attempt to come to joint convictions about when collective work products make more sense than individual ones.

EXERCISE 7.3
Working Out Different Metrics for Assessing Outcomes

Explore different ways to evaluate progress and success against specific collective work products, with respect to the overall mission and purpose of the team. Again, use breakout groups to expand on the ideas and increase the number of different options that could be effective tracking and measurement mechanisms.

EXERCISE 7.4
Designing and Conducting Different Meetings for Different Purposes

Design and conduct a meeting that is focused entirely on individual reports and efficient use of time. Design and conduct a meeting that is focused entirely on collective work products, problem solving, and solution design. Design and conduct a meeting that can serve both purposes. Draw on some of the ideas and approaches detailed in Chapter 4.

EXERCISE 7.5
Testing the Members' Understanding of Desired Outcomes

Ask the members to describe the overall mission and purpose of the group and the most important end products and outcomes. Evaluate those descriptions with respect to terminology, time frames, and metrics. Identify inconsistencies, confusion, and disagreements. Break into subgroups and discuss ways to close the gaps.

EXERCISE 7.6
Evaluate the Language Used by the Group

Ask different members of the group to keep track of the language that is used in meetings. Evaluate that language with respect to how people refer to goals, tasks, and activities. How often are the terms *we* and *us* employed versus *me, you,* or *they*? Use breakout groups to construct a common language dictionary of critical terms that capture important meanings and behavior patterns. Identify and discuss whether the group falls into "either/or," "win/lose" debates versus "both/and" integrated dialogue and discussion.

CHAPTER 8

Obstacles and Opportunities for Virtual Teaming

Groupware is not automatically teamware . . .

There is good news and bad news for virtual performance units. On the positive side, groupware can help people in multiple locations and time zones collaborate more effectively with one another without creating insurmountable logistical, expense, travel, and scheduling difficulties. Groups can also save their work more easily than ever before. They can introduce new members and ad hoc contributors to the group's purpose, goals, approach, and progress. Members from anywhere in the world can link into *virtual team rooms* that embody and enhance the quality, effectiveness, and efficiency of the group's work.

On the other hand, groupware poses many new and different challenges. In fact, just getting members to make use of the appropriate groupware options can be a challenge in itself. And, there is a potential dark side to the technology. Horrendous stories of e-mail proliferation are perhaps the most familiar illustration of what can happen to human interaction when technology gets out of hand. Other challenges exist as well. Foremost among them, as reviewed in Chapter 2, is acting as if groupware replaces or changes the two basic disciplines of team and single leader for effective small group performance. In addition, small groups that rely so much on groupware that they fail to meet with one another physically can sacrifice the emotional commitment, shared understanding, and mutual respect critical to team performance. Last, but not least, there are the challenges of keeping conversations private so that they are open and constructive, and keeping the number of participants small enough so that members do real work together.

Both the positive and negative effects of groupware arise from three fundamental characteristics of the technology: (1) expanded access, (2) asynchronous participation, and (3) disembodied communication. When combined, these realities make the work of virtual groups both easier and harder at the same time. Clearly, the most important point we make in this section is how groupwork technology reinforces natural biases toward the single-leader, instead of the team, discipline, often at the expense of performance results.

The rest of this chapter divides the positive and the negative aspects of the three technology characteristics cited above into two parts: (1) the consequences of expanded access, and (2) the consequences of asynchronous participation and disembodied communication. We conclude the chapter by describing the impact of globalization on all three characteristics.

Expanded Access

Groupwork technology enables greatly expanded access to people, documents, discussions, metrics, and even access to the past. As long as the hookups are in place, your team can

tap into the knowledge, expertise, and participation of anyone inside or beyond your company; and anyone can tap
into the work of your team, both as it is happening and as it
is saved. It is possible, in fact relatively easy, for everyone
involved to read documents, participate in discussions, calibrate progress and metrics, and stay abreast of whatever work
the team can capture and do within the medium of the technology.

On the positive side, this vastly expanded access is effective, efficient, and powerful. More information, awareness, and participation stimulate better performance. For example, we know a team that was responsible for developing
and implementing a new strategy in a global enterprise. In
the course of writing their plan, they sought help from a
consultant familiar with their company's culture. Without
groupwork technology, this team would have had to spend
days briefing the consultant prior to meeting with him. The
effectiveness of the briefings would have depended on the
respective memories and rough notes of the team members
about what they were trying to accomplish and what work
they had already done.

With groupware, however, the consultant could easily access and read through the saved work of the team, including
threaded discussions, documents, metrics, and other materials collected at the team's site. (For a review of groupware,
see Chapter 2.) When combined with phone conversations,
groupware permitted the consultant to learn how the team
had approached their challenge. Moreover, the consultant
could use the groupware to post comments in threaded discussions and make suggestions regarding critical issues and
documents, all prior to any face-to-face meeting with the
team.

In other words, the interaction between the consultant

and the team was immediate, comprehensive, and time-efficient. Critical, shared understanding was developed before the consultant ever met with the team. The consultant customized his advice in ways that would not have been possible without groupware and within a fraction of the time it would have otherwise taken to do so. When the consultant finally met face-to-face with the team, everyone had a richer understanding and perspective about the challenge at hand. Hence, the whole group focused their time together on the most critical issues. As one member commented, "The meeting was half as long and three times more effective. . . ." This was because of groupware.

What happened in this example can and should happen regularly with teams who seek counsel or input from others through the medium of groupwork technology. As discussed in Chapter 5, teams often must seek help from ad hoc contributors, sponsors, or other people who do not have to become fully committed members of the team to make meaningful contributions. Groupware facilitates the assistance of such people.

At the same time, however, expanded access poses difficulties. To begin with, large numbers of people complicate and hinder *both* of the small group disciplines we are discussing in this book. With such unlimited access, small groups must be careful not to get too large. When groups are too large the single-leader and the team disciplines do not work well. The team discipline demands a small number; teams that get much larger than ten or twelve rarely succeed unless they work in subgroups. Groupwork technology too easily causes teams to collapse under the strain of involving too many people.

The negative impacts on the single-leader discipline are also apparent. Decades of organizational behavior and effectiveness research have shown that the ability of one leader to stay in control breaks down as the number of direct reports gets up into double digits. In such instances, leaders delegate responsibility to others to hold the span of control to a manageable size. But as authority gets delegated, organization complexity grows. And while manageable spans can vary considerably under different conditions, there is always a limit to the number of people one leader can oversee. Groups that deploy groupwork technology in ways that precipitate excessive growth in the size of the group are well advised to consider sub-teaming options, or "rules of engagement" that clearly differentiate between core team members and ancillary contributors. Large groups of people need to move beyond the scope of the two performance unit disciplines in order to accomplish their objectives.

In addition to size, groupware has a number of other, less obvious impacts on small group effectiveness. True performance units, especially those applying the team discipline, always develop an ethic of accepted and unaccepted behaviors for collaboration. For example, many teams emphasize fact-based discussions that are open to all ideas, but not personalized toward anyone on the team. This kind of ethic emerges through trial by fire—the "storming" well known to anyone that has teamed with others. "Storming" leads to "norming" as key, behavioral expectations and rules are set by the group. Effective teams conclude that: "We can and should disagree constructively within the team. But we need to keep our disagreements and 'dirty laundry' inside the team."

Keeping disagreements "in the team" is jeopardized when the discussions of the team are available to others. Teams that use advanced groupware and fail to discuss an approach for dealing with this difficulty run two serious risks. First, a person who is not a mutually respected, legitimate member of the team can gain access to storming discussions. Intentionally or unintentionally, this access can spread negative controversy and mistrust within and beyond the team. Second, people on the team lose their candor in groupware discussions because they question the security of the arrangements.

Consequently, groups must openly ask and answer questions about the role, contributions, and access to the team's work by ad hoc contributors and others beyond the team. Think for a moment about working in a familiar, physically co-located team. You would not invite every ad hoc contributor to every team discussion. Yet, unless virtual teams are careful, this is what happens with groupware. Members are strongly inclined toward inclusion and openness for the sake of broadening the information base. As valuable as such broadening may be for information purposes, it can easily inhibit team performance when it weakens or threatens mutual trust among the core members. It is critical to ask such questions as, "Will this person be a fully committed and mutually respected member of the group? And, if not, what restrictions do we impose regarding access to the team's ongoing and saved work? What restrictions, if any, will be imposed on his or her participation in the team's current and future discussions? What norms or rules must he or she follow? And how can those norms be enforced without losing valuable inputs?" It is often constructive to engage the ad hoc contributors in answering these questions.

Asynchronous Participation and Disembodied Communication

When small groups meet face-to-face or over the phone, they participate synchronously, that is, they interact at the same time. Much of groupwork technology, however, allows for asynchronous participation, i.e., most members working at different times from different locations. To illustrate, let's say that on Tuesday afternoon you post the draft of a document for an upcoming operating review, and on Wednesday morning I e-mail comments to you. Later on Wednesday, you review my comments, make a few changes to the document and repost it. I scan the document for your changes on Thursday. This is purely asynchronous participation, that is, you and I are never discussing the document together at the same time.

Moreover, in this example, our communication is entirely in writing; we are not talking with one another. Our communication is disembodied, literally stripped of body language, facial expression, and vocal tones. I read and responded to your document and you similarly responded to mine. At no point do we discuss your document while we are together in the same place or at the same time. My input is limited to what I read in your words and vice versa. If I should misread your tone or intent, our reactions can get off track and become dysfunctional. Even if we add telephone interactions to this situation, we are still handicapped in our ability to interpret important thoughts, feelings, and meanings that are not carefully and explicitly articulated.

The effects of asynchronous participation and disembodied communications are best understood in combination. The good news is that efficiency rises when you and I are not tied down by the logistical necessity of working on the document at the same time and place. Even more important than the costs and inconveniences associated with logistics (e.g., scheduling a time and place when we are both available, which, if we work in different cities, might mean expensive travel) are the increased possibilities for more constructive reflection and input. In the synchronous case, you and I would review your document at the same time in one anothers' presence. One or both of us might do a less thoughtful job because of pressures surrounding our moment of interaction. Perhaps I am running to catch an airplane or have just left a difficult meeting. Perhaps one or both of us cannot absorb all the implications of the document in one sitting. Perhaps we only think of important comments later when it might be too late or inconvenient to contribute them.

Groupwork technology also enhances the contributions by people who might not feel entirely comfortable or confident in group settings. Remember that e-mail, threaded discussions, and electronic data dissemination are relatively stripped of status. As a result, people who might not speak up for reasons of hierarchy, job role, or personality in synchronous meetings often feel comfortable doing so within the protection of groupware. Moreover, the body language and facial expressions present in physical meetings can reduce participation. How many times have you or a colleague been inhibited from speaking by the combined tonal and facial grimace of another group member making it clear that "this is not the best time to speak up"?

Finally, input from group members can receive a fairer hearing when read by others asynchronously and without the attendant body language of the group. This is one of the most commented-upon phenomena in the World Wide Web: when we consider comments without knowledge of status, position, hierarchy, gender, race, ethnicity, age, or other criteria, we focus more on content and substance. We are less inhibited by extraneous factors and find ourselves being more open-minded. In such cases groupware clearly enhances the possibilities of better thinking, better decisions, and better work.

Yet, in addition to the many advantages of asynchronous

participation and disembodied communication, there are three serious disadvantages:

1. Groupwork technology can limit group creativity. Teams that fail to have face-to-face interactions diminish their chances for spontaneous collaboration. We have all attended sessions when people built on one another's ideas in exciting and unexpected ways. *This kind of group creativity arises from being physically present.* Groupwork technology enhances the possibilities in two important ways: (1) each individual's contribution will reflect his or her individual very best thinking, unimpeded by pressures of time, place, or presence of others; and (2) each person will receive the best, fairest hearing from other members of the group. Yet, it comes at a cost. Groups often do their most creative and critical work *as groups* rather than as individuals. Through working together in the same room at the same time, they generate insights and creative solutions not likely to emerge from asynchronous, individual contributions.

   As we pointed out in *The Wisdom of Teams,* the stories of successful teams invariably turn on some critical juncture or moment when the team—*as a team*—jelled around an idea or an event or a possibility. The odds of such creative and vital moments decrease when all the work and interactions of the group happen in cyberspace. With groupware, you each may interact well and work constructively with each others' words and documents, but that is not the same thing as working and collaborating with the entire group present.

2. Groupware can subtly convert collective work products into individual work products. To understand how, we

need to look closely at co-location. Even though the word literally means *same place,* co-location actually involves two aspects: place and time. Obviously, if you and I are working together in the same room, we are collaborating at the same time. But, you and I might be connected over the phone or in a chatroom and be working together at the same time, even if not in the same place. In each of these two cases, we are doing work together. But when we rely strictly on asynchronous features of groupware, for example, see the document revision process discussed earlier, we are not performing co-located, collaborative work together. We are more like relay runners, each taking the baton from the other before doing our individual work, and passing the baton back. Groupware may shorten the time intervals between baton passes. But asynchronous individual effort, regardless of how often and efficient, cannot replace working together when simultaneous interaction and nonverbal communication is required.

Teams that ignore this subtle distinction between working together versus working individually do so at their own peril. They discover too late that their collective work products have become a series of individual work products.

For example, a team from STMicroelectronics set a goal of breaking company records for the time it took to bring new products to market. They used groupware to assemble programmers, designers, and others from India, France, and California. The team assigned collective work products to programmers and designers from all three locations, which spanned more than ten time zones.

They learned that merely calling something a collective work product, however, did not lead to true collaboration through the medium of groupware technology. Because of the radical time zone differences, those assigned to the group tended to rely on groupware to the exclusion of face-to-face or even synchronous voice interactions. It is extremely difficult to schedule and hold teleconference calls spanning the time zones that stretch from India to California. As a result, essential aspects of collaboration became impossible. For example, the programmers from India literally had coding conventions that went unexplained to their colleagues in France and California.

The team eventually recognized that collective work products demanded co-location. At critical junctures, they chose to fly people from India to France and California and station them there until the needed progress happened. A rough rule of thumb emerged around the question, "How many times must team members interact with one another during the day in order to make progress?" If the answer were greater than one or two, it was a sure sign that co-location, or at least reasonably finite time zone differences, had to be established.

3. Groupware technology endangers mutual accountability. Asynchronous participation and disembodied communication combine to threaten the shared understanding and emotional commitment demanded by the team discipline's requirement of *common* purpose, *common* goals, and *commonly* agreed upon working approach. Recall the discussion in Chapter 6 regarding common versus compromise and consensus. *Common* requires a demonstrable, shared understand-

ing of purpose, goals, and approach; in contrast, *compromising* to achieve consensus too often reflects some ill-founded imperative for 100% agreement. Shared understanding, without 100% agreement, typically requires a lot of group work that comes from effort as a group instead of only from a series of one-to-one interactions with each others' written words and documents. Of the dozens of virtual teams we have participated in or observed, it is not surprising that none could succeed without meeting early on as a group to discuss team basics. Nor was it surprising to find that such discussions were equally necessary whenever the team got stuck or faced a particularly difficult challenge.

The aforementioned elements of expanded access, asynchronous participation, and disembodied communication are all increasingly common in today's global environment. Seldom do we encounter a company with any significant growth potential that is not giving a high priority to operating in multiple parts of the world. Manufacturing operations find lower-cost labor abroad, sales efforts cannot resist new markets overseas, and investors are constantly seeking the untapped potential of global resources. As a result, small groups of all kinds are working across global boundaries with a regularity and diversity seldom experienced just a decade ago.

Simply put, there is no other way for such groups to perform without dealing in some way with the elements of expanded access, asynchronous participation, and disembodied communication. Added to that is the complexity of different language and cultural barriers that must be overcome. English may have emerged as the "language of business." But, while many Europeans, Asians, Africans, South

Americans, Middle Easterners, and others from around the globe are articulate in English, their cultures are very different, making nonverbal communications difficult to interpret even in face-to-face situations. Moreover, unique cultural heritages can dramatically affect small group performance. In Germany, for example, there really is not a commonly used term for *team;* hence, the English version is usually applied. In Japan, the importance of a strong leader is a cultural norm that literally defies team basics.

Most groups that aspire to team performance among members from different cultures find they need to create a *team culture* of their own, rather than try to get all members to subordinate their behaviors to reflect any single cultural way (e.g., the "American" way or the "German" way or the "Japanese" way). The emergence of such team cultures is more common within global organizations where strong values already cut across national boundaries. McKinsey and Company is an excellent example of a truly global enterprise that has a set of values that enables multicultural groups to work together effectively.

Still, performance units in any culture or nationality are primarily a matter of applying the right discipline to the performance task at hand. In those countries where strong leader behavior is more firmly ingrained in a national culture, you are more likely to encounter single-leader units within that country's enterprises. At the same time, however, the potential value of team performance is real, although the effort required to achieve it may be much harder.

It is no accident that *The Wisdom of Teams* has been translated into fifteen languages and has continued to be a best seller overseas for nearly ten years. Nor is it any accident that we continue to receive unsolicited testimonials from members of teams all over the globe. Virtual teaming technology merely accentuates the importance of multi-cultural groups becoming proficient at the two performance unit disciplines. But, multicultural groups must pay especially close attention to the concerns we cite regarding the effects of expanded access, asynchronous participation, and disembodied communication.

Bias Toward the Single-Leader Discipline— The Distortion of "Working Together"

The expanded access, asynchronous participation, and disembodied communication characteristics of groupware bias groups toward the single-leader discipline. Whenever the performance goals of the group are best achieved through the single-leader discipline, this bias is constructive. But if your group faces challenges that demand the team discipline, then you must be careful to recognize and deal with the bias of groupwork technology.

Ironically, most groupwork technology claims to contain "tools for teams." Yet, a careful look at project management, threaded discussions, document management, and executive management features reveals their bias toward individual work and individual accountability. Think about your own experience with such technology. When you are working—whether responding to email, posting a discussion item, reviewing a document, checking progress on metrics and goals, or making or receiving a task assignment—you are working *alone*. You may be interacting with the words of others. Unfortunately, interacting with another person's words is not the same as interacting with the whole person in real time. Without the benefit of body language, facial expressions, and tonal innuendo, you can easily miss the intent, if not the entire point, of an important communication.

As discussed in Chapters 1 through 4, collective work products constitute a powerful litmus test for identifying team performance situations. The need for the team discipline is high when tangible results must be delivered by two or more people collaborating in real time. But, there is a bias in groupware technology toward using the single-leader approach. If we are not careful, we expect people to collaborate on a collective work product, but, like the STMicroelectronics team, encourage the opposite. The way they conduct their actual work tends more toward individual work, responsibility, and accountability. In an all too typical response, one person with long experience with virtual work efforts clearly indicated that, on reflection, he had rarely worked in virtual groups that assigned two or more people joint accountability for work products and goals; a telling illustration of the bias of this technology toward individual accountability. Instead, he said, the prevailing pattern was "one person, one task."

This systematic inclination toward individual work and individual accountability reinforces the biases of consequence management. As discussed at length in *The Wisdom of Teams*, most managers have much more experience and confidence in using the single-leader discipline than the team discipline. Effectively using groupware to apply the team discipline, then, demands more rigor and conscious deliberation about when to team. Otherwise, you will not avoid the traps associated with the bias toward individual work products.

What to Do: Practical Pointers on Virtual Teaming and Virtual Work

Before reviewing best practices in virtual teaming, let us repeat our central message: *Do not take your collective eyes off performance and how best to choose and use the single-leader and team disciplines to achieve it.* As you move forward, here are some critical steps you and your group should consider:

1. Use face-to-face meetings to build and develop shared understanding and commitment, as well to get un-stuck. Such meetings are important early on when the group is beginning to develop the mutual respect and understanding required to succeed. Equally important, however, are those times in a virtual effort when things are not working and the group is stuck or becalmed. Often the best, and sometimes the only, way to get back on track is to work together in the same room at the same time. Groupwork technology can certainly re-duce, but rarely eliminates, the need for face-to-face in-teractions over the entire course of a demanding per-formance challenge. One comment echoes many we have heard: "We bonded [only] when we met in per-son." Effective team performance, of course, is not pri-marily about bonding. But without meaningful, face-to-face interactions and doing real work *together,* it is extremely difficult to build understanding, respect, and accountability for a team's purpose, goals, and working approach. Yes, in that unusual instance when a group of people are well-known to one another and have worked together a number of times, we can imagine effective teaming without any face-to-face interactions. In fact, we encountered such a situation at General Electric's electric motors business in Fort Wayne, Indiana. A key member of a leadership team in Fort Wayne was physi-cally located in Singapore where the unit's manufactur-ing operations were concentrated. Many virtual team efforts by the group were successful without his physi-

cal presence, but largely because he was so well-known to his other teammates. Such circumstances are the exception rather than the rule in today's workplace. And the more complex the group challenge becomes, in terms of both performance results and location/time zone diversity, the more frequently face-to-face sessions make sense.

2. Avoid the illusion of collaborative groupware meetings. To some extent, this is a corollary of the point just made. Whenever teams gather through groupware to advance, they need to recognize and adjust for the key differences between face-to-face and groupware interactions. In Chapter 4, we cautioned against approaching all meetings in the same way. We encouraged readers to recognize when meetings would benefit from a concern for time-efficiency versus providing for a more open-ended, problem-solving approach. Groupware interactions work well for the first, but are problematic for the second. Nonetheless, in the course of a virtual team effort the group must often use groupware to enable open-ended, problem-solving sessions. Accordingly, we encourage teams to recognize the constraints imposed by technology and consider the following aids: (1) explicitly appoint facilitators, (2) use chat features simultaneously with voice or video, (3) carefully poll members whenever a particularly critical subject arises, and (4) apply any other technique the group can imagine to make sure that dialogue remains open-ended.

3. Do not swamp yourselves with high numbers. From the beginning, your group should discuss what it means to be a full member of the group versus a partial member

or contributor. Unlimited involvement is not the name of this game! You must choose deliberately and consciously who will have access to what. You need to establish special protocols or access codes to implement these decisions. You should establish clear criteria to delineate core group members, and thereby enable you to control the size of your group. As the number of people making contributions to your team grows with the passage of time, you need to regularly review the status of each person as *core group member* versus *partial contributor.* Make whatever changes are merited, including limiting or eliminating access to the group-work technology by those whose roles are no longer core or who have completed their assignments on your behalf. Finally, if the number of ad hoc contributors gets too large for the group leader to oversee, create subgroups and divide up the oversight responsibility among other core members of your group.

4. Discuss and decide which features of groupware you will use and how you will use them. Like most software and hardware, groupwork technology continually improves, with more and more features and functions added all the time. Today, your group has access to hundreds of features and functions. As a result, far too many groups make two critical mistakes. First, they fail to deliberately discuss and choose which of the features to use and exactly how to use them. Second, they overestimate the number of features and functions the group can effectively master in the early phases of teaming, and, as a result, create frustrating and confusing technological interactions. (Even in the writing of this book, for example, the authors utilized

incompatible software for several weeks before appropriate modifications could eliminate the frustration.)

Instead of careful deliberation and choice, groups
too often participate in broad, generalized training or
install groupwork technology with vague and unrealistic expectations about skill, knowledge, and familiarity.
For example, you assume I am familiar with threaded
discussions and post a comment. When I don't respond,
you get frustrated. When this happens, groups quickly
learn to use only those features with which each person
is already familiar (e.g., e-mail alone). This lowest common denominator approach seriously underutilizes the
technology. And the attendant frustrations and confu-
sions delay the effort. In contrast, groups who deliberately choose which features they will use tend to ensure
common understanding and shared learning about
those features.

If you are relatively new to groupwork technology,
start with only a handful of features. That way, your
group can develop skills, usage, and familiarity together. As a few features are mastered, others can be
added. Do not, however, force a shift in groupware without full group support, assuming that the advanced capability will somehow carry the day. Use the exercises in
Chapter 2 to help your group learn to pick and practice
the groupware features that make the most sense to
your performance challenge.

5. Discuss and choose your own *netiquette*. Chapter 6, describes the importance of agreeing on the common
working approach to be followed by your team. You
need to meet face-to-face early on to agree on several

things: (1) how you will divide up the work itself; (2) how you will administer yourselves and deal with logistics; (3) what approaches should be used for decision-making and evaluating progress; and, finally, (4) what behavioral norms, or rules of the road, will be required. Your group should discuss each of these with reference to groupwork technology. If you will rely extensively on groupware, an explicit discussion of the expectations and anticipated use regarding that technology ought to be an integral part of your working approach.

For example, you need to deliberately choose whether everyone connected with your effort or only core group members receives e-mail or are otherwise included in threaded discussions and document sharing. What are your expectations regarding input? Must you hear from all members on each critical document and issue, or only some members? What about language? Will your group welcome jokes? Will you tolerate *flaming* (i.e., harsh invectives aimed at people inside or beyond the group)? What about participation itself? Will your group set an expectation regarding usage of the groupware technology? Or, will you permit usage to rise and fall without any expectation?

When your group faces a critical choice or decision, how will you work together? It's a good idea to identify some conditions that will signal the need for face-to-face work. For example, what kinds of collective work products are likely to require face-to-face participation? Since you probably cannot meet face-to-face for every decision, what kind of participation will you encourage or expect prior to decisions? Who will make the decisions and on what basis or with what contribution from others? How will you communicate those decisions to one another? Will you communicate them to ad hoc contributors or other people beyond the extended group in you organization?

6. Discuss and assign monitoring and guiding roles regarding the group's use of groupwork technology. Groupware demands new leadership roles, especially with regard to project management, document management, and threaded discussions. In each case, someone should be formally assigned to pay attention to whether the work of the moment, for example, discussing and resolving an issue or reviewing and improving a document, is getting done in the manner best suited to performance.

   In some ways, this required role is analogous to a facilitator, gatekeeper, or leader in face-to-face meetings. For example, imagine that six of us are assembled to review a document. We would ensure the document has been read before the meeting and is reviewed thoroughly by all of us at the meeting. We would seek comments from everyone at the meeting, trying to ensure we took advantage of our individual and collective best thinking. As the meeting drew to a close, we would agree on next steps and responsibilities for any required redrafting of the document and set a time for the next review.

   This approach is clearly familiar, but as with so much in groupwork technology, it takes on a different spin when the meeting is not face-to-face. One or two people in your group must take responsibility for ensuring that the document in question receives comparable input, agreement about what might be changed, and assignment of next-step responsibilities. If such roles are not explicitly assigned and communicated, the required work often falls through the cracks.

Put differently, your group needs to assign people to be discussion guides and administrators. Someone must pay attention to whether group members are using the groupwork technology, participating in document management and threaded discussions, responding to e-mail and other alerts, getting their tasks done, submitting needed metrics and other information, and so forth. And if anyone is falling short, the guide or administrator needs to communicate on-line or off-line to find out why and what can be done to improve participation and contribution.

Do not assume that the person assigned this role must be the group leader. Nor should you always give this role to the same person. Groupwork technology permits your group a lot of flexibility in assigning such roles. Like the other suggestions made in this chapter, however, you must make such choices and assignments explicitly and self-consciously. Again, this is best done face-to-face. Groups who assume that groupwork technology will run itself are heading for trouble.

7. Pay particular attention to when and how to shift the leadership role in situations that require team performance. One of the great strengths of the team approach lies in shifting leadership to fit the task at hand. Doing so, however, is challenging for any small group aspiring to team performance. But it can be even more difficult in virtual teaming because of the strong bias towards the single-leader discipline.

For that reason, it is critical that the formal leader of a virtual team situation engage the core team actively and extensively on this topic. Develop clear guidelines for when and how to shift the leadership role. A performance agenda, like that discussed in Chapter 4, can guide virtual teams through the thickets of shared leadership.

Review and use the exercises in Chapter 2 after reading Chapter 8. In addition, consider the following:

EXERCISE 8.1
Role Definition and Access

Once your group has selected the features and functions of groupware you will use, spend time distinguishing the access to your group work that will be given to full members versus partial members. You might need the help of technologists to implement the decisions you make. Once you have put your decisions into practice, review how effectively they are working and make the needed adjustments. Also, schedule a regular review of who has what access so that you can prune, add, and modify scope of access whenever needed.

EXERCISE 8.2
Netiquette

Once near the beginning and then again after a few weeks or so of experience, your group should set netiquette rules of behavior and expectations. These include answering the following questions:

1. Are people expected to check the team's site regularly? If so, how regularly?

2. Are there time limits for responding to people? If so, what are they, and are they limited to only certain kinds of issues or alerts?

3. Is there any limit to the kind of language your group wishes to impose?

4. Who gets alerted on what kind of issues?

5. Will you monitor usage of groupware by team members? If people are falling short of usage, what are the consequences, if any?

EXERCISE 8.3
Calling for a Face-to-Face Session

In advance, your group should fully explore the circumstances under which anyone in the team can suggest or call for a face-to-face session. By identifying the parameters for calling them and formally discussing and reviewing such sessions, you will learn when and how to use these critical moments for group progress.

EXERCISE 8.4
New Member Introduction

Whenever a new member or ad hoc contributor gets introduced, ask one or two people from the team to prepare an appropriate introduction guide and package. This package ought to include a description of the group's performance challenge, goals, and work plan; a description of the kind of contribution expected from the new person; access to the people and backgrounds of people on the team; and, most important, access to the *relevant* saved work of the team that is critical to the role of the new person. For example, ad hoc contributors should have access to those particular threaded discussions, documents, and other work that will quickly and effectively provide them the background they need.

EXERCISE 8.5
Guide for Guides

If you are assigned the task of guiding discussions and other aspects of groupwork, then you need to choose how you will perform each of the following critical tasks:

1. Monitoring threaded discussions and other forms of participation.

2. Posing questions to relevant members on relevant subjects.

3. Polling group members on key issues and decisions.

4. Ensuring that people have read and responded to documents.

5. Attending to disagreements and ensuring they become enlightened instead of unenlightened. (See Chapter 6.)

6. Contacting members either on-line or off-line when their participation and contributions fall short.

EXERCISE 8.6
Collective Work Products and Co-Location

Using Exercises 1.5 and 3.5, identify and assign collective work products critical to the performance of your group. Now ask those assigned to determine the opportunities and impediments they foresee in applying groupware technology to their work. Ask them to pay particular attention to the number and nature of daily interactions required for success. Determine if the number of interactions is significant and/or if the nature of their collaborative work demands face-to-face approaches to working together. If so, ask the group to figure out a work plan that builds in the appropriate co-location, together with a budget for the related logistical expenses.

CHAPTER 9

Getting Unstuck

We are getting nowhere fast!

The road to getting "stuck teams unstuck" is paved with good intentions. Groups that set high goals and strive to apply the discipline of team basics encounter all kinds of obstacles that thwart their progress, erode their commitment, and frustrate their initiative. Of course, the easy way to avoid getting stuck is to simply ignore team basics and claim togetherness as a victory. Unfortunately, that's exactly what many small groups do; it is a lot easier, but they do not achieve team performance. A second way to avoid getting stuck is to call yourself a *team*, but apply the single-leader discipline; it is faster and more comfortable. However, when you face an important real-team challenge, the single-leader discipline falls short.

The bad news is that groups find it nearly impossible to avoid *getting stuck* when attempting to work as a real team. To begin with, real teams are hard work because they set demanding targets and have to work in unnatural patterns. As a result, they invariably encounter unforeseen obstacles that prove difficult to remove, get over, or work around. In the process, the team gets stuck.

The good news is that being stuck can be one of the best things that happens to a team for three reasons: (1) the members learn a lot about one another and their challenge as they struggle together, (2) surpassing the obstacle builds confidence and strengthens commitment among the members, and (3) the group improves skills and enriches its working approach for dealing with future obstacles. Hence, as Julie Sackett of Motorola's Government Electronics Group reminded us in *The Wisdom of Teams,* ". . . it is good for teams to stay stuck for awhile." At the same time, however, teams that stay stuck for too long erode and self-destruct. To avoid that end, it is important to understand:

1. Why teams get stuck in the first place.

2. Options for getting unstuck by letting the members *work it out.*

3. Options for getting unstuck with outside intervention.

4. When and how to end team efforts that can't get unstuck.

Why Teams Get Stuck

Teams get stuck, or run into trouble, for lots of reasons. In the course of our work with teams over many years, we have encountered and heard about dozens of different problems that well-intentioned team efforts have faced. Some were common and predictable; others were unique and unpredictable. In the second edition of *The Wisdom of Teams,* there is an appendix that chronicles over 50 specific questions that were raised in our discussions with working teams after the book's publication in 1993. These questions and answers highlight many causes of stuck teams. Our purpose is not to repeat that level of detail here, since it is probably impossible to develop a complete list of things that block team efforts.

Instead, we will describe six fundamental reasons why teams run into trouble. While certainly not all-inclusive, we believe these six encompass most of the causes for stuck teams. At the heart of them all is the failure to make a conscious choice to apply the discipline of team basics with rigor and consistency. Sometimes that failure arises from contrary attitudes and behaviors among the members, sometimes it is precipitated by leaders and sponsors of the team, and sometimes it is driven by forces outside the control of either the team or its sponsors. Most of the time, however, we have found that teams and sponsors can get the team unstuck by simply working on the basics.

The six fundamental reasons for stuck teams are:

1. *Unclear goals:* Because team performance relies on members pulling in the same direction, confusion about targets and goals invariably bogs down the team. These targets must include the overall performance purpose and outcome-based goals, plus the milestones and time frames when key end products must be delivered. Every team situation calls for a different set of targets. And how targets get set can vary from team to team. For example, some teams take their targets from sponsors; others set targets themselves. In addition, many teams start with a clear set of targets, but as the work progresses, priorities can change; hence, targets also need to change or confusion results. The better

teams consistently revisit their targets *as a group* to ensure clarity and common levels of commitment among the members. As long as people on the team can demonstrate a shared understanding of their targets and have worked to establish team ownership of the targets, then the clarity required ought to emerge. Thus, the first vital sign to check when your team gets stuck is target clarity.

2. *Mistaken attitudes:* The most important attribute for a team leader is an attitude best expressed as, "I believe our challenge is really important, but I'm not sure how best to accomplish it; hence, I really need the help (i.e., talents, skills, initiative, and insights) of every member." This is quite different from the strong group leader who says, "I know what needs to be done here, how best to get it done, and will hold each member personally accountable for accomplishing what I assign."

   Correspondingly, the attitude of each member of a real team is best expressed as, "I am part of a very important performance effort that requires the skills and leadership capability of every member; I respect and know we need the full capability of each of my teammates." This differs significantly from, "My role is important, I have the right skills, I know what my assignment is, and I will carry it out regardless of what others do," and, "It's the group leader's job to get the necessary contributions from others."

   The attitude that must prevail throughout the team, of course, is that no one or two members of the team can be blamed if we fail because we are all in this together. This attitude precludes finger-pointing and cross accusations when trouble strikes. Without that attitude, the commitment, collective work products, and shifting leadership that teams require cannot happen, and the team will either get stuck or underperform.

3. *Missing skills:* The primary advantage that a team brings to a performance challenge is its ability to integrate the multiple skills and talents of all its members to produce results beyond what is possible through individual effort alone. The required skills are a function of the performance purpose and the goals and work products. If the right sets of talents are not present among the members, and it is unrealistic to expect the missing skills to develop within the group, the team cannot accomplish its purpose or mission. No amount of determination, initiative, and hard work will compensate for a missing set of talents and critical skills. For example, you cannot develop superior software products if you don't have team members who can write great code.

   In leadership teams, a problem is often created because the required *working skill* does not reside within the team. In other words, the membership is determined more by position or title than by necessary working skill. Unless the working approach of the team provides for the addition of the right skills, many issues cannot be effectively addressed. For example, developing a marketing plan for penetrating the Korean market for fast foods requires a team member who understands what kind of foods Koreans eat.

   Sometimes, of course, missing skills and talents can be provided by individuals who are not permanent members of the team. There are many ways to access particular skills for short periods of time or for specific end products (temporary or part-time contributors, outside consultants, etc.). However, if a particular working skill-set will be required throughout the team's efforts on several of the collective work products, that skill set or the potential for developing it should be reflected in one or more of the permanent members of the group.

4. *Membership changes:* Often the membership of teams that function over several months will change. Whenever a new member is added to the team, the other members, along with the leader and sponsors, need to work to integrate the new member. In some ways, this is equivalent to reforming the team, since it is essential that the purpose, goals, and working approach be agreed to, internalized, and committed to by the new as well as old members. It is not unusual for this process to result in some changes to the goals and working approach, since new members bring fresh ideas and perspectives. When a group does not allow time for this kind of involvement, discussion, and integration, the new member may not develop the same level of commitment, thereby weakening the team. Also, the time required to integrate new members can in itself cause the team to lose momentum or get stuck.

   If the team leader is changed, of course, the task can be even more difficult. And sometimes, if the leader lacks the right attitude, the team not only becomes stuck, it requires a complete restructuring.

5. *Time pressures:* As mentioned earlier, time is often the enemy of a group that seeks team performance, particularly when that group has not yet acquired team skills and has members unfamiliar with the basics of the

team discipline. Shaping a performance purpose, a set of outcome-based goals, and a working approach that are based on common levels of commitment of all members of the team requires more time than the single-leader discipline. This time trade-off is most evident in the formation of the team, but it is also a cause of teams getting stuck or diverted.

When time pressures become severe, a group that has not yet mastered the discipline of team basics will invariably revert to single-leader behaviors to expedite its process. This change can be constructive and appropriate when all members of the team understand the rationale for that shift in behavior, adjust to it, and then shift back into team mode when time permits. Unfortunately, many groups embarked on a team effort are disrupted by a time-driven shift in behavior and strongly resist the leader's intervention.

6. *Lack of discipline and commitment:* In the end, team performance is much more about discipline and commitment than it is about empowerment and togetherness. The six elements of team basics must be applied consistently and rigorously across the changing landscape of the team's mission. Any erosion or lack of attention to any of the six basics will confuse, if not derail, the team. Certainly, a primary role of the leader is to apply and enforce the team discipline. However, leaving it to the leader or sponsor is not good enough. Team members often must rise to the occasion to discipline one another. And in the final analysis, the role of self-discipline by each member is perhaps the most important of all. In short, the team discipline must be applied

by the leader, by other members, and by the individuals themselves.

There is a risk, of course, that a command and control attitude on the part of the team leader can supercede a balanced, three-dimensional enforcement of the discipline that arises from leadership pressure, peer pressure as well as from within each person. When that happens, the group either reverts to a single-leader unit, or it will resist and stop progress until the rationale is understood and accepted. The team discipline works only as long as the leader's discipline efforts are supported by the members and vice versa.

Regardless of the environment and context for team efforts, all teams experience periods of frustration, resistance, and getting stuck. Teams that stay stuck too long will lose heart and commitment; they revert to compromise units and perform at low levels, if at all. Hence, it is very important to recognize the likelihood of getting stuck, and for all members to have a common understanding of why the team is stuck. Once that understanding exists, it is usually possible for the team members to work through the problem and emerge stronger than before. When a stuck team cannot work things out among themselves, however, outside intervention can help. When neither of these options work, it is time to radically restructure or terminate all teaming efforts.

Options

Working It Out

Of course, one approach to letting the members work it out is somewhat analogous to locking them in a room until they emerge with the solution. A classic old movie, *The Dirty*

Dozen, depicts just such an event. A well-known actor, Lee Marvin, plays the role of a maverick army captain who has been assigned the impossible task of transforming 12 soldiers serving life sentences (convicted, hardened criminals) into a specialized guerrilla team to carry out a dangerous mission behind enemy lines. Early in the group's formative efforts, a violent disagreement breaks out among the 12, and a fight ensues. The captain (to the amazement of his top sergeant) simply leaves the room, locks the door, and lets the group fight it out. They did not instantly become a team, but they did develop a healthy respect for each others' fighting skills that helped them as they learned to work as a team in order to survive their mission.

Sometimes *locking the door* works in real life, too, but more often than not it is better to guide the direction of the *work-it-out* effort beyond the fight-it-out approach of *The Dirty Dozen.* The most natural starting place is to revisit team basics and conduct a simple group assessment to identify gaps in the discipline:

1. Are we all clear on the performance purpose of our effort, and can we all describe what success will look like in similar terms? If some of us see success differently, it is time to spend serious time in *purposing discussions* to narrow or integrate our differences.

2. Are team goals stated in terms of outcomes rather than activities, and do we all agree on the goals and their relative importance? If not, it is time to launch more goal-setting, clarification, and prioritization sessions.

3. Is the team's working approach clear to all, and does that approach still fit the circumstances (i.e., both the tasks to be done and the constraints on the time and

role of each member)? If not, it is time to rework our approach against whatever constraints now exist.

4. Does the group have the right sets of skills for the goals and working approach? If not, should we consider adding new members or finding ad hoc or other special contributors? Or, can we make work assignments to build the needed skills?

5. Does the group have a clear way of holding itself mutually accountable? If not, or if members view accountability factors differently, the group must clarify responsibility and accountability and how they will be assessed.

6. If we are a virtual team, are we making the best use of groupware without falling victim to its disadvantages? Is it time, for example, to hold a face-to-face meeting to discuss and resolve outstanding issues and problems? Do we, perhaps, need to increase the frequency of face-to-face meetings to achieve team performance levels? Have we shaped collective work products that, instead, are being worked on individually instead of collectively? Do we have too many people participating in what ought to be the exclusive work of full team members? Do we need to reshape our rules of engagement with respect to ancillary contributors versus the core team?

Revisiting the basics usually clarifies what might have slipped. If, however, a serious revisiting of the basics does not lead to a clear picture of the cause of the trouble and pinpoint a solution, the group must consider a more rigorous assessment of the situation. Injecting a fresh perspective and new information can help. Too often, groups make careless or uninformed assumptions about being a team, when, in fact, there is no performance reason to pursue that option. Another example of a common assumption that misleads a group is, "We should behave as a team all the time, or at least whenever we are all together," when, in fact, there are important tasks for the group to attend to that require clear, strong direction from the formal leader and individual responsibilities and contributions. These kinds of assumptions are a form of *denial* of what the actual performance task requires. As long as that kind of denial dominates a group's thinking, it is difficult for members to assess the appropriateness of their behavior. Self-assessment and correction help best when the performance task, as defined by both outcome-based goals and working-approach specifics, is rigorously evaluated separately from the behavior pattern of the team.

Unfortunately, most existing team self-assessments make the mistake of assuming that team behavior is always better, that is, that a real team will somehow be the right answer for any group performance challenge. An important exception to that pattern was developed recently by Niko Canner of Katzenbach Partners LLC, working in conjunction with Southwest Airlines and BMC Software. This computer-assisted instrument enables teams to assess their performance situation separately from their actual behavior. It also helps them clearly distinguish *effective group behaviors* from *disciplined performance unit behaviors,* and thereby pinpoints the specific areas where behavior change is warranted by performance goals and challenges. Figure 9.1 illustrates how 27 teams at Southwest Airlines used the device to categorize their situations relative to their behavior. Note how explicit positions on the chart highlight different options for moving toward a higher level of performance.

Another important option for teams having trouble mak-

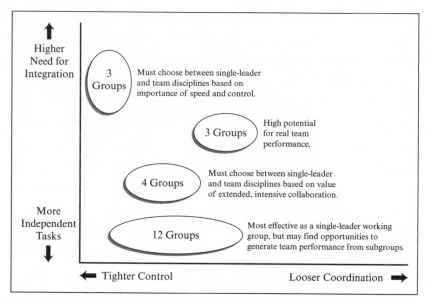

FIGURE 9.1 Distribution of group challenges—airline client samples

ing reasonable progress, even after a rigorous self-assessment based on fresh information, is to consider a shift in their agenda that can permit them to go after more doable performance goals. A few tangible accomplishments, or quick wins, can do wonders for a group's confidence, as well as give members a chance to practice different behaviors under less pressure. For example, if the team is stuck trying to find ways to increase their sales penetration of large accounts, they might decide to turn their attention to a smaller account or to target a smaller and easier segment of the large account. Anything that is a bit easier to achieve provides an opportunity to get the group back into a positive frame of mind, as well as to sharpen team skills.

A final option for getting unstuck requires dealing with obstructive or ineffective team members. If one or more members are clearly the cause of the blockage and resist all attempts to get them back on track, it may be necessary to change one or two members. There are two ways to accomplish that. The most straightforward is simply replacing the recalcitrant member(s) with someone else. But teams do not always have the latitude to replace members assigned by higher authority. In such cases, it is possible (although never easy) to find ways to work around noncontributing members. *The Wisdom of Teams* describes such a case with the Enron deal to steel team of fifteen official members, thirteen of whom found a way to work constructively around two non-contributors.

Outsider Intervention

Outsider intervention should not be the first place to turn when your team is stuck. Rather, you ought to turn to this option only after exhausting efforts within the team. There are, however, several ways to obtain outside help. Adding new members can bring new perspectives, experience, energy, time, and skills. But, as described earlier, whenever teams add members, they need to go through some kind of reforming in order to incorporate the new without losing the commitment of the old. Give and take is absolutely essential in this process if the new members are to contribute fully and develop comparable levels of commitment to the team's purpose, goals, and working approach. Unfortunately, this takes time. The group needs to revisit its purpose and goals and readdress its working approach to integrate the new members. You cannot simply hand them a statement of your purpose and goals and expect their commitment and full understanding. Nor can you simply ask them for any suggestions and expect to get the full benefit of their fresh viewpoints. In fact, teams that do this best usually take several working sessions to accomplish the integration. (Although, as reviewed in Chapter 8, groupware technology can facilitate this process.)

When the new member is a team leader, the challenge is even more significant. Existing teams do not often accommodate new leaders easily. Indeed, they regularly find themselves resenting the fact that one of the existing members was not given the leadership opportunity. In our research for *The Wisdom of Teams,* we encountered one such example at Hewlett-Packard where senior management imposed a new leader on the team. It took the team more than a year to work itself back to a level of real team performance. In retrospect, it might have been better to replace the former leader with one of the existing team members, as had been strongly recommended by the outgoing leader.

Nevertheless, bringing in a new leader is sometimes just what a stuck team requires, particularly when the team has exhausted the efforts of its leader. If the team has been effective in the past, then the incoming leader should tread carefully. Real teams are proud of what they have accomplished, and, because teaming requires shifting leadership, most members have led the team in important tasks in the past. And while, on the one hand, they may welcome a new leader who can get them unstuck, they are likely to feel a bit self-conscious about not being able to surpass the obstacle themselves. Strong leaders who have never led real teams represent the biggest problem here, since they presume that the single-leader discipline is best and might believe that the source of the problem was the former team leader's lack of decisiveness. Once again, a key to the effective introduction of a new leader can be found in the new leader's ability to quickly and rigorously assess the performance situation. When, in fact, performance calls for the single-leader approach, the leader should go that route. But when performance demands the team discipline, the leader needs to take the time to re-form the team around a common purpose, common set of goals, and commonly agreed upon working approach. Most important, the new leader must also find ways to shift the leadership role to others without losing the formal mantle of leadership.

Introducing an outside facilitator is another common method of intervention. Unfortunately, it can easily become a crutch for weak groups who really should be working things out for themselves. When facilitators are effective, they tend to be both experienced observers of group interactions and behaviors as well as strong, performance-oriented problem-solvers. They can often help the group identify causes of serious blockages that are not clearly perceived by the members. Moreover, outside facilitators are sometimes better able to confront behaviors and attitudes that are counterproductive to team performance, particularly when they help conflicting team members turn unenlightened disagreement into enlightened disagreement and choice. (See Chapter 6.)

Team or more accurately, perhaps, effective group training, can be a valuable outside intervention, provided the training is customized to the specific performance challenge facing the team and is delivered with astute attention to team basics. Far too many well-intended training efforts actually emphasize group dynamics rather than team basics and performance unit disciplines. As a result, the training clouds the horizon with dozens of issues that are not at the heart of achieving team levels of performance. Thus, rather than help the team get unstuck, the training further complicates the situation. Another problem with so-called team training is that it is often targeted to the early formation of small groups and the broader concepts of group learning. In short, it fails to focus on a stuck team's particular performance challenge, problem or need, and it fails to focus on the critical choice between team and the single-leader unit disciplines. Nonetheless, a well-designed team workshop that allows the members to workout their problem and situation within a team-basics training framework can be an excellent way for a stuck team to get unstuck.

A final option for outside intervention involves sponsors or higher level of management. Whenever team leaders or members need to be replaced, sponsors and higher level managers usually become involved, although they may not actually initiate the action. In fact, it is usually best if team members themselves come to the realization that an injection of new talent is needed. Not surprisingly, the higher level intervention that works best comes from sponsors who are very close to the team, recognize its past accomplishments, how and why it is stuck, and can intervene in ways that are consistent with the level of commitment that needs to be maintained. It is particularly valuable when the sponsor recognizes the difference between an effective group and the two disciplined performance units. (See Figure 1.1.)

There are, of course, ways for well-informed sponsors and senior management to intervene that are very helpful and that do not involve replacing members or team leaders. A sponsor can help by participating actively and constructively in one or more team-work sessions where he or she helps with the real work of the team but does not take over the session or preempt the role of the working leader. A sponsor can locate and help provide access to missing skills, talents, and new perspectives. And higher level managers can arrange for self-assessments by the team or provide outside facilitation. Last, but not least, a sponsor who is also an experienced team leader can provide helpful one-on-one coaching for new team leaders or members who are unaware of problems they may be causing the team. In fact, stuck teams will sometimes encourage their leader to talk with the sponsor about the team's problems with the legitimate expectation that such coaching will occur.

Terminating the Effort

"Know when to hold 'em, know when to fold 'em," goes an old poker player's adage captured in a song made popular by Kenny Rogers. You can waste a lot of time, money, and energy trying to get team performance out of a group that is hopelessly stuck. Struggling to resurrect a dead team is painful for everyone involved, particularly the team members. Learn to recognize the signs that usually mean a stuck team is a dead team:

1. A team leader who cannot give up control and cannot be replaced. Some leaders just cannot abandon their ingrained preference for calling the shots, even when counseled, coached, and commanded to the contrary. The fundamental attitude imperative to team leaders ("I *need* this team") is just not possible here; so if replacement is out of the question, you should terminate all efforts to promote real team performance.

2. Recalcitrant team members who cannot be circumvented or replaced. Sometimes you can work around, or replace, a recalcitrant group member and sometimes you cannot. When such members stand in the way of team performance, and there is no way to work around them, they will continually derail team efforts. It is better not to try.

3. One or more team members whose primary commitment is elsewhere. For real team performance to occur,

it is essential for all members to be committed to the purpose and goals of the team, above all other commitments. When a team member continually demonstrates primary allegiance to another source that diverts his attention from critical team tasks, it is time to work around the obstacle or find another way.

4. A group challenge that does not require any important collective work products. It is surprising how often groups who believe in teamwork continually strive for team performance when no required or significant collective real-work opportunities exist. Again, this desire can waste the time of a number of people. Without clear team tasks and collective work-product goals, team efforts cannot achieve team levels of performance and should be avoided.

5. Inability to build or obtain critical skills. A lawyer cannot provide the anesthesia for a heart transplant team; they must have a competent anesthetist. Otherwise, the surgical team cannot carry out the operation successfully. As obvious as this analogy seems, we are continually surprised to find groups who try to achieve very demanding team goals despite the insurmountable absence of critical skills and talents.

6. Members with critical skills that cannot lead the group. Occasionally, a person with exactly the right set of skills will be unable to lead the group in an area of expertise. When all attempts to get such members to step up to this challenge fail, it is time to look elsewhere.

7. Time pressures that will not yield. Sometimes there is just no time for teaming, particularly with a group that has not worked as a team before. When that time pressure is more important than the collective work product

and team performance opportunity, it is much better to use the single-leader discipline.

In short, there is no point in banging your head against an immovable stone wall. Any of the above conditions might preclude real-team levels of performance. As soon as you are convinced that one of these conditions exist without any hope of changing, it is time to terminate the team effort and move on to other approaches.

Many of the ways to get teams unstuck have already been described and captured in exercises throughout this book. They fall into some obvious categories of effort that require little more than simple awareness of the option. Others, however, are much easier described than applied. Hence, the following useful exercises, tools, and techniques:

EXERCISE 9.1
Purposing and Prioritizing Workshop

Design and conduct a one- or two-day workshop that refocuses the group on its overall performance purpose by identifying and prioritizing the key issues it faces. This workshop should be preceded by a series of individual interviews, usually by someone who is not a member of the team, where the members can, in a confidential setting, identify what they believe to be the key issues facing the group, both with respect to their working approach and the achievement of their performance goals. It is usually helpful to ask someone outside the team to conduct the interviews and the workshop discussion. It is critical that this outsider has as much orientation toward performance goals and disciplines as toward group dynamics and behavior.

EXERCISE 9.2
Cross-Learning

Create two- or three-person subgroups to interview one another about why they are members of the team, what skills and experiences they hoped draw on, and what seems to be precluding the optimal use of their skills and interests. Then have each subgroup report back to the group as a whole, protecting personal confidences, and discuss how to better utilize the skills and perspectives of the team to achieve performance.

EXERCISE 9.3
Active Listening Exercise

Conduct a working session where each member is required to repeat back any individual communication from another member. Then the other member corrects the listener until the communication is right. This session often benefits from the input of an experienced facilitator at first to make sure that members understand how they are to respond. (Use the approach to enlightened disagreement discussed in Chapter 6.) Be sure to focus on communicating about the purpose, goals, working approach, and obstacles facing the team.

EXERCISE 9.4
Coaching Tools and Techniques

Pair up within the team, and get each person in the pair to provide coaching to one another; again, in a confidential mode. It is surprising how effective untrained coaches can be when given a protected opportunity where everyone is expected to give and receive personal coaching. Obviously, some difficult cases will benefit from more professional coaching, which can also be provided for in this exercise.

EXERCISE 9.5
Role-Switching

Set aside a one- or two-day working session, and purposely shift the roles, both leadership and critical skills. Each person is to work for two hours in the shoes of the other members. Ideally, every person will fill the role of at least two other members during this session.

EXERCISE 9.6
Self-Assessment Tools

Break the group into subgroups, and have each subgroup do an assessment of how they see the group functioning against one or two of the six elements of team basics (see Chapter 1). Have the subgroups report back, and then have the group as a whole do an overall assessment. Consider the use of computerized self-assessment tools to enrich the specificity and quality of the assessment. The latter is particularly valuable in assessing the performance situation separately from the behavioral and interaction situations. Always remember to start any team assessment effort with a rigorous evaluation of the performance tasks it will face. Do these tasks require a team or not?

EXERCISE 9.7
Sponsor and Team-Leader Workshop

Where multiple teams are involved, it can be useful to convene a workshop only for the sponsors and leaders of the various teams. In this kind of session, different team experiences can surface, and sponsors and leaders can learn a great deal from one another.

CHAPTER 10

Teams and Change

Change and change again

Every organization that expects to compete and grow must deal with change. Not exactly "new news," is it? Human institutions have confronted change challenges for centuries, some more successfully than others. The magnitude and pace of change, however, is considerably more daunting today than ever before. As a result, leaders throughout organizations put ever-higher premiums on teams because, as we discussed at length in *The Wisdom of Teams,* teams are an essential building block for performance in the face of profound change.

Small group performance capability built on the combined use of the team and the single-leader disciplines is no longer a "nice-to-have" option for enlightened leaders in pursuit of empowerment; it is a necessity. Largely because of the overwhelming amount of change we all face, performance challenges demand that small groups adapt and respond quickly in all parts, places, and levels of the enterprise. Yet, most small groups continue to fall short. Instead of continually developing their capability to adapt and perform, too many small groups get stuck in the single-leader discipline. Or, when they attempt teaming, they do so in the name of togetherness instead of performance. Instead of disciplined performance units, they remain, at best, effective groups. It is always easier to promulgate teamwork and advocate teaming than to ensure team performance. As a result, understanding when, whether, and how to use the team discipline—"in harness" with the single-leader discipline—to deliver small-group performance is essential to success in almost every sector of the world economy.

This chapter is devoted to clarifying the roles of both small-group disciplines in inducing change. To that end, we divide this discussion into two major sections: one-time change that creates a significantly *new platform* of performance capability and ongoing adaptive change that sustains a *moving platform* of competitive capability. Both kinds of change benefit from both disciplines, although in somewhat different ways.

One-Time Major Change

Enterprises periodically find themselves in need of a major human effort to restore, maintain, or catapult to new levels of competitive effectiveness. Sometimes this is the result of falling behind in a changing marketplace, or of a technological surge; sometimes it is the result of completely unexpected and unpredictable discontinuities. The Justice Department's decision to break up Microsoft is an example of the unexpected; although some might argue that management should have considered its change options months earlier.

Few organizations are forever immune to these one-time, major upheavals, no matter how clairvoyant and enlightened their leaders may be. Over the years, we have seen that major change efforts divide themselves into two categories: *decision-driven* versus *behavior-driven* change. (See Douglas Smith's *Taking Charge of Change*.) In the decision-driven group are those changes that, extensive and important as they are, can move forward on the backs of critical choices and decisions alone. Perhaps a merger or alliance is enough; or, bringing in a new CEO; or, developing a new product. Decision-driven change demands a tremendous amount of leadership and hard work, particularly at making and communicating the decisions and translating those decisions into performance. But decision-driven change is never as difficult or as challenging as behavior-driven change.

Behavior-driven change, too, requires decisions. It is just that decisions alone are seldom enough, regardless of how well-syndicated, communicated, "bought into" and reinforced. If your company faces a major change where, in order to implement the tough decisions, you have a significant number of already-employed people that must learn specific new skills, behaviors, and working relationships, then you face behavior-driven change. You must have a critical mass of real change leaders in the middle and near the front line, as well as change leadership at the top. Leading behavior-driven change is one of the most difficult challenges on the planet. Consider five of the more obvious examples of behavior-driven change:

1. *Front-line operating groups:* Some of the most difficult challenges of one-time change efforts are confronted at the front line. When the skills and behaviors, and some-

times even the basic talents, of front-line workers need to change, it takes more than compelling admonitions from the top. Team performance plays a critical role in such efforts because, typically, teams excel at determining what has to change, designing the programs and mechanisms to guide the change, and energizing hundreds of people to attempt it.

Front-line change comes in many forms. Service-based companies, such as KFC and Marriott International periodically must develop and build different skills among entry-level workers in order to respond to shifting market needs; they cannot hire enough new people to replace all those with skill gaps. Their problem is one of retaining, retraining, and educating, rather than attracting already-skilled people from untapped sources. These situations invariably rely on teams because teams are uniquely good at both delivering outcome-based performance goals and learning new skills. Specially created frontline teams or task forces can identify and clarify skill needs within major segments of the enterprise, as well as focus multiple-team efforts on learning new skills.

2. *Key account sales groups:* One-time change efforts among sales groups have similar problems. Increasingly, industries as widely divergent as professional services, information technology, retail banking, and telecommunications, have discovered what has been the case with industrial marketing for decades: It takes a small, cohesive group of experts from a variety of different functions to penetrate, sell, and hold an account. When the marketplace dictates a significant, step-function change in skills and behaviors within

these groups, the team discipline becomes imperative. True teammates know how to work together to share knowledge, experience, and customer perspectives. They help one another build and enhance individual skills, as well as create new group capability. New skills and talents can be integrated into existing teams when team basics are adhered to. Selected members from real teams also can be deployed temporarily into ad hoc efforts to further shape and design the changes and support requirements across broad segments of the sales force. But, whatever specific tactics are tapped, shifting a sales effort from the individual-as-hero approach to the team approach involves behavior-driven change.

3. *Product and service design and commercialization groups:* A dynamic marketplace can pose significant behavioral and skill challenges to product design and commercialization efforts and to all of the people who must contribute to them. Gone are the days when companies could safely and confidently innovate new products once every few years. Today, the cycle time from new idea to first purchase has dropped radically in telecommunications, information technology, automobiles, clothing, pharmaceuticals, financial services, and retailing, among others. Winning enterprises have learned that innovation and new product and service introduction efforts are particularly helped by the team approach. Rapidly changing technology also requires major rebuilding of capabilities and approaches in critical product and service design and commercialization groups. In the latter case, it is often necessary to introduce new talents who understand the emerging tech-

nology and how it will affect product design and service requirements. Again, to the extent that real-team capability already exists, it can be a great advantage. Ad hoc teams can be deployed to evaluate and promulgate the full implications of marketplace and technological change. Ongoing teams can quickly digest the new knowledge and put it to use in designing and delivering new product and service offerings that beat competitors to the punch. This understanding can be more readily introduced into a multiple-team environment because of the learning and adaptability of real teams.

4. *Major program and/or business management groups:* A common example of a behavior-driven change occurs when a large, functionally organized enterprise restructures itself. Usually, the purpose is to increase significantly the number of business units, or major programs, that will have full profit responsibility and can make decisions more responsive to the marketplace. Too often, however, the leaders of the restructuring effort discover that the number of tested general managers is short of the need. For example, corporations with an historic pattern of functional management provide limited opportunities for people to develop the integrative skills of a general manager. Hence, these skills will be in short supply, and developing them will represent a major challenge. For the new organization to deliver performance, lots of existing leaders have to rapidly learn new behavior, skills, and ways of working with others. Almost inevitably, the new business units that succeed are led by executives who tap into the power of the team discipline to expand leadership capacity and performance at the top.

5. *Special leadership projects:* Unfortunately, there are relatively few examples of successful major change efforts
   that have encompassed large multi-business corporations. Most of those, however, were designed and or-
   chestrated by special performance units, real teams
   and single-leader units, that formed at several levels of
   the enterprise. Often, such units are commissioned and
   set apart to lead their special efforts over the course of
   several months. Sometimes these are full-time assignments; sometimes not. The list of such efforts is as long
   as the special demands of performance and the imagi-
   nation of effective leaders. It includes reengineering,
   quality, innovation, e-commerce, diversity, corporate
   citizenship, best place to work, customer or marketing
   orientation, alliances, strategy, and more. In our experience, there is a direct correlation between the use of the
   team discipline and the success of such efforts. In fact,
   we cannot think of a single example of a special major
   change initiative that succeeded in the absence of applying the team discipline as well as the single-leader
   unit discipline.

Of course, there is always the danger of overdoing the team
aspects of major change. If everyone involved is assigned to a
team and the effort itself becomes obsessed with teaming,
then many of the small groups involved will fall into the trap
of treating *team* instead of *performance* as the primary objective. The single-leader discipline is as critical to change as the
team discipline. And if teaming for the sake of teaming is
stressed, the consequence will be compromise units and
failed change. As with most challenges, however, the risk typically run is that groups will select either the single-leader discipline or the team discipline to the exclusion of the other,

when, in fact, performance demands the wisely integrated application of both. When this happens, the actual performance delivered by these various small groups and special project efforts falls short because:

1. They don't always get team performance where it counts; unfortunately, getting *teams at random* is not good enough.

2. Too few people clearly understand and apply the two performance-unit disciplines with discrimination and rigor; unfortunately, undisciplined teaming efforts destroy the performance potential of both teams and single-leader units.

3. Personal favorite styles of leadership prevail, and managers become satisfied with effective group efforts; unfortunately, costly and frustrating compromise units proliferate.

Don't make these mistakes. If you are involved in any of the major change efforts described here, pay particular attention to the performance objectives and goals of your small group and how you can use each of the two disciplines best for success.

Adaptive Change

In a perfect organization, one-time, major transformational change would never be necessary. A truly responsive and adaptive enterprise would anticipate marketplace dynamics and respond in ways that sustained a competitive advantage without any need for catch-up efforts, such as The Home Depot responding to Lowe's and other building supply imitators. The workforce in such organizations would be comprised of talented and adaptable people who learned whenever and whatever made the difference to ongoing success. For example, Hewlett-Packard evolved from 57 diverse technological measurement units into a few integrated pools of computer businesses. Even major, unforeseen discontinuities would not create gaps beyond the grasp of the adaptive and flexible enterprise; the way that Microsoft will need to respond to the threat of a government-mandated breakup. Such is the essence of the high-performing organization that endures over time.

Unfortunately, this ideal organization has never existed. But, there have been several organizations who have enjoyed long runs at such adaptability. And the ideal itself is a worthy object of management focus, attention, and aspiration, so long as it is directly linked to performance. Indeed, the companies who sustain superior competitive adaptability over time tend to be companies who have a maniacal focus on delivering performance results to multiple constituencies (e.g., customers, shareholders, employees, and alliance partners). It is when organizations seek adaptability for its own sake that they get in trouble.

Any organization that focuses so clearly on performance that it can avoid one-time major change will be an organization where the team discipline is well understood and applied. Teams are the single, most powerful unit for delivering both performance and change. Why? Because people who need to apply the team discipline to meet specific performance challenges are people who must learn some new way to collaborate or acquire a new skill in order to succeed. Again, recall the circumstances under which performance is best attempted through the single-leader discipline. It is when performance itself can be achieved through the sum of individual best efforts. Certainly, such circumstances might call for individual learning, but not always. In marked contrast, real team members invariably learn from one another. As we stated in *The Wisdom of Teams,* we have never seen a team challenge that did not require some form of new learning and change that benefitted all members. Never. And in the decade since *The Wisdom of Teams,* that observation has not changed. Teams remain the single best vehicle we know that inevitably demand both performance and change. Consequently, they are as critical for organizations seeking to remain adaptive as they are for those who do face one-time, major change.

Avoiding the Extremes

As already noted, the extremist *either/or* point of view about teaming versus the single-leader discipline is counterproductive, if not dangerous. To make the inevitable teaming capability used during one-time, major change an ongoing part of the adaptive organization will not happen by managerial instinct or individual consequence-management. Instead, most organizations also need to generate mechanisms to perpetuate and wisely apply the team discipline. But, team-based paradigms and lofty teamwork pronouncements seldom result in team performance where it counts. Such notions invariably lead to one or both of the following extremes: (1) team overload, where the overemphasis on teaming produces a preponderance of costly, compromise units; or (2) team resistance, where leaders purposely avoid teaming in the name of enforcing individual accountability.

Organizations, no matter how well designed and led, do not ensure team performance in the right places by advocating teamwork or eulogizing teams. Indeed, the very idea of a team-based organization is naïve. It fails to answer the demands of ongoing adaptability: Instead of linking the team discipline to performance, it separates the two. Teaming becomes the objective itself and causes harm instead of good.

When senior leaders announce their intention to become a team-based organization, they almost always generate an intensive communications effort pointed on *becoming a team* and *being a team.* They label all small groups, and some large groups, teams. In effect, they act as though they are flipping a light switch. "We are no longer a command-and-control hierarchy built on a solid foundation of single leaders and individual accountability; henceforth, we are all a team." The misleading implication of this well-intended but impractical pronouncement is that an empowered, team-based organization is what produces the infinitely adaptable organization. But nothing could be further from reality.

Just as successful, one-time major change demands different kinds of mechanisms and tools, so does the mastery of perpetual and adaptive change. A managerial system that excels at responsive, adaptive change exhibits three characteristics with respect to teams:

1. A set of values that encourage both team and single-leader performance units

2. The collective leadership ability to choose wisely and consciously integrate both performance units into a truly balanced leadership approach

3. The discipline to assess performance, as well as behavior, and fit the solution to the need

Shaping Discriminating Values

Values are the beliefs, behaviors, and attitudes that determine and describe "the way we do things around here." Every organization has a set of values, although not all are explicitly stated and some are established by default. The more clearly values are understood and followed throughout the organization, the stronger its culture and the more consistently it can perform, *so long as its culture is consistent with the demands of performance.* The stronger a culture, the more difficult it is to change. Hence, it is imperative to build responsiveness, adaptability, and discipline into the culture and values of any organization that expects or aspires to deal with constant change.

Because teams are the most flexible and adaptable performance unit, team capability is extremely important in mastering adaptive change and continuous learning and improvement. It follows that those values that support and nourish the team discipline, the single-leader discipline, and the use of performance itself to make the choice are also values that will generate and sustain adaptability. In our experience, the following values are key:

1. A strong, commonly held belief in focusing on and delivering performance; not change for the sake of change

2. An understanding that performance begins with specific, SMART outcome-based goals; not amorphous activity-based goals

3. An understanding that performance includes both financial and nonfinancial indicators and encompasses a balanced scorecard; not a narrow focus on shareholder gain that subsumes customer value, employee fulfillment, and other critical stakeholder benefits

4. Strong, demonstrable beliefs by leaders at all levels that there are two disciplines, not one, for small-group

performance; not simply consequence management based on individual accountability alone

5. Beliefs, behaviors, and attitudes on the part of leaders at all levels that they and their group should look to performance itself in making the choice of when to use the single-leader discipline and when to use the team discipline; not relying blindly on personal favorite approaches

6. Demonstrable beliefs and attitudes on the part of team leaders that they really need the efforts of everyone on the team to succeed and that when the team discipline is used, the team must be in control; not simply one leader plus "a few good men."

Making Conscious Choices

We have stressed throughout this book how critical it is to make the choice between the team and the single-leader discipline a conscious, deliberate one with reference to specific performance challenges and goals. In Chapters 1, 3, and 4, we provide a set of tools, a framework, and exercises to help. Still, after a decade of writing about and working with small groups, we continue to see far too many leaders and groups who assume that their natural instincts about management are good enough. Such leaders and groups do not consciously choose which discipline to apply to which performance challenge. They seldom even press beyond the notion of *effective groups* to pursue the power of performance units. As a result, such leaders and groups fall short of delivering optimal performance.

Organizations that aspire to move beyond this lazy pattern

must find ways to demand, encourage, and support conscious choice-making in small groups. The simplest approach, of course, is to regularly require and review the making of the choice itself. Managers with one or more separate small groups and the small-group leaders reporting to the managers should regularly work with the groups to determine which of the two disciplines they should apply to their performance challenges and why. Building a challenging review of such choice-making into regular management interactions will powerfully reinforce the kind of skills and behavior required for a disciplined approach to performance, as well as adaptability.

Assessing Performance and Behavior

The most common failure among leaders who aspire to change but fall short is sticking with *what works* in situations that demand different approaches. "If it ain't broke, don't fix it," or "Dance with the guy what brought you," are mindless shibboleths that people use to rationalize their strict adherence to what they have previously found most comfortable.

Unfortunately, change, particularly adaptive change, demands the opposite. You cannot wait for things to break, nor can you dance only with the person you find most comfortable, and expect to stay at the top of your game. An absolute bias toward what has worked before and what is comfortable will cause problems in adaptive-change situations. Important options will be overlooked, valuable tools will be ignored, and critical change challenges will be poorly addressed. As a result, disciplined adaptability will remain out of reach.

On the other hand, if what has worked before will continue to work, you should stick with it. Once again, performance is at the heart of things. Adaptive change is all about maintaining the capability to outperform the competition despite dynamic and unforeseen marketplace developments. Hence, it is essential to assess behavior and skill patterns against performance itself. Change leaders cannot simply assume that every task is better accomplished by a teaming effort. Nor can they assume that their personal favorite leadership approach can conquer every challenge that comes along. They must use a rich toolkit of individual and group approaches.

Any small group pursuing adaptive change, therefore, should be diligent about assessing its performance tasks, as well as its behaviors in relation to those tasks. To that end, there are several proven guidelines, or rules, for making team performance an integral part of a balanced, change-adaptive organization:

1. Keep performance the primary objective. Don't be led astray by the desire to team for its own sake: a sure path to the dreaded compromise unit. If you do need to apply the team discipline, however, don't. Focus on performance results. Teams are all about achieving performance results through collective work products, mutual accountability, and shared leadership. Those must remain the primary purpose, objective, and underlying rationale for the discipline itself.

2. Start small and build team capacity one step at a time. Broad-based, all-at-once teaming efforts sound good. But they never work. Instead, they confuse people into focusing on teaming generalities instead of performance specifics. Emphasizing the broad generality rather than the explicit discipline leads to costly overkill. Far better to proceed carefully and diligently by adding team efforts only as fast as you can ensure that

the discipline of team basics will be rigorously applied in the right place at the right time.

3. Deliver training, education, and other assistance *just-in-time* to small groups rather than individuals. Don't waste money and resources on broad-based training efforts that troop scores of individuals through workshops and seminars. These efforts may produce effective groups, but not performance units. Instead, train teams as teams, and only train those teams that need to apply the team discipline to a specific performance challenge. Better yet, wait to deliver training until teams identify particular gaps or challenges. By taking this "just-in-time-to-perform" approach, you will help teams address problems, obstacles, and resistance in real time. The more focused and timely, the more likely the assistance will accomplish its purpose.

4. Integrate teaming initiatives along with other change initiatives. Launching a team initiative on a stand-alone basis is likely to fail. Why? Because it inevitably implies teaming for teaming's own sake as the primary purpose. Consequently, first determine whether you face a significant change challenge that will demand the increased skill, hard work, and application of the team discipline. Only then should you launch a teaming initiative. And that initiative should be carried out in close combination with the one or more specific performance initiatives that truly require the changed behaviors or skills that you seek to impart. Team and change initiatives will feed on one another, thus multiplying the momentum and performance benefits of both.

5. Set outcome-based performance goals for team support efforts. Training, information, and other assistance

should be measured against the same kinds of outcomes that are required of teams. In other words, judging the success of the support system by the raw number of teams or individuals who are trained is not good enough. Success of the support efforts must be traceable to performance results or outcomes not activities.

6. Enforce a common language that differentiates the team and single-leader disciplines. Language always matters to successful change. People and organizations who are undisciplined about the key words, phrases, and other language that capture and pinpoint change requirements, fall short. Consequently, the language we have emphasized throughout this book is language that you can rely on to produce performance and change, if you remain vigilant and disciplined. If you invest your collective time and attention in learning and applying the language of *the team discipline, the single-leader discipline, outcome-based goals, six basics of the team discipline, performance agenda, behavior-driven change, decision-driven change, I, we,* and *performance,* you will go a long way toward winning. These distinctions matter.

7. Create a critical mass of change leaders who differentiate between the team and the single-leader disciplines and successfully apply both. Teams are the most flexible unit for driving change, but they are not the only unit. The most effective small-group efforts in any change effort are those that use both disciplines with equal facility. The more leaders you can grow who are comfortable, confident, and experienced in both disciplines, the more adaptive your organization will become.

Following these principles will not guarantee a more effective integration of team performance into an overall, balanced performance capability. It will, however, increase the odds of successful integration and guide your efforts to strengthen the performance capacity of your organization.

Many of the exercises and tools that have been described in earlier chapters are also appropriate in addressing change challenges. In addition, we find the following six exercises to be particularly useful:

EXERCISE 10.1
Shaping a Common Language of Change

The purpose of this exercise is to create a common language to capture the essence of the change and highlight critical distinctions. Start by brainstorming a list of terms and short phrases that characterize *what will be different* if change is successful. Make a similar list of what will be different. Develop a list of terms and phrases that describe new tools, mechanisms, and techniques that will be essential to introduce and master. Break your group into subgroups, and develop new definitions for these key terms, comparing them specifically with the current definitions that will need to be changed. Finally, pick the most significant five to ten terms, and develop a reminder wallet card or desk plaque for each member of the group, and possibly broader distribution to others that you will be working with outside the group. Remember, as always, to explicitly discuss why these words and phrases matter to performance.

EXERCISE 10.2
Mapping Informal Networks

Identify the three or four most important informal networks that need to be a part of the change effort. For example, a cross-unit communication network, a change process advisory network, a knowledge/expert network, and a decision syndication network. These may be networks that already exist, but will have to be modified significantly for the change to take effect. Assign two or three people the task of *mapping* each of the networks you have identified. This can be done in successive levels of detail (i.e., first, from personal knowledge; second, by interviewing others who will occupy key nodes in the network; and third, by conducting a detailed survey of those most affected by the network). Each subgroup should develop a preliminary map of the network assigned and lead the entire group in a discussion of how its network will affect their efforts and success as a group going forward.

EXERCISE 10.3
Identifying and Prioritizing Pivotal Groups

The purpose here is to identify the five or six small groups that will be most critical to your change effort. In any major or adaptive change effort, literally hundreds of small-group efforts come into play. Obviously, some will be more important than others—and the relative importance will shift over time. Start by listing the specific groups that have an impact on the change and performance to which you aspire. Determine whether each group identified will need either or both the team and the single-leader disciplines. Decide how to interact with those groups, and identify specific relationships that need to be developed.

EXERCISE 10.4
Climbing the Branches of the Y

Review the Y introduced in Chapter 1. This concept helps teams clarify and develop common perspectives about the flexible approaches and behaviors they need to match their behaviors to the performance tasks they face. The purpose of this exercise is to focus your attention on the key distinctions between an effective group effort and the two more disciplined performance units. Start by developing a list of the ten to twenty outcomes that will be required of your group. Obviously, this should already have been accomplished in the initial goal-setting efforts of your group. Once the list is agreed upon and clear to all, break into three subgroups. Assign one group the job of completing the base of the Y (i.e., outcomes that require only effective group behavior to accomplish). Assign a second group the job of completing the left branch of the Y (i.e., outcomes that require superior single-leader discipline). Assign a third group the job of completing the right-hand branch of the Y (i.e., outcomes that require the team discipline). Reassemble the entire group, identify areas of overlap and disagreement, and problem solve until you have completed the Y to everyone's satisfaction.

EXERCISE 10.5
Conducting Round-Robin Role Changes

The purpose of this exercise is to develop greater facility among the group in playing different roles. Begin by identifying the different roles that members must play in accomplishing the group's purpose. Do not, at this point, identify or assign particular roles to particular people. You should be able to define at least a dozen different roles that are important to achieving your goals. For example, there will be con-vening/leadership roles for different topics, communication roles for different audiences, support roles for different situations, problem-solving roles for different types of problems, etc. Once the roles have been agreed upon, identify the most natural or obvious choice for each role, based on past experience. Next, identify three, outcome-based tasks or issues that the group needs to address, and address each one with members consciously playing different roles from the ones they might normally play. Once the three tasks have been accomplished, convene an overall group session and discuss how the role changes affected the results and how the group can become more effective when role changes are essential.

EXERCISE 10.6
Clarifying the Points of Change Resistance

The purpose of this exercise is to understand the sources of change resistance that must be dealt with and devise approaches for doing so. Draw a large matrix on a chart or wallboard with one axis defining levels of the organization as well as key individuals or groups and the second axis defining functions of the organization. Problem solve as a group or in subgroups to describe the points of resistance within each of the cells of the matrix. Rank these points of resistance in terms of potential disruption to the effort and degree of difficulty to overcome. Discuss possible strategies and approaches for dealing with the most important points.

Wisdom is Discipline

This book begins and ends on the same note: Team wisdom is applying the right discipline at the right time. It seems simple enough, but as any small group intent on higher performance knows, it is a lot easier said than done. In fact, it is invariably more acceptable and comfortable to work at the effective group level, label yourselves a team, and let it go at that, thereby avoiding all of the frustrations of trying to: (1) establish a clear performance purpose, (2) agree on outcome-based goals, (3) carve out a working approach that integrates skills and shifts leadership roles, and (4) find practical ways to hold one another mutually accountable. These challenges require hard work.

When an effective group isn't good enough, it is second nature for us to anoint a strong leader who will instinctively apply the single-leader discipline and enforce individual consequence management. Unfortunately, instinct and second nature will seldom produce real-team performance when and where it counts; you have to make conscious choices. As a result, wisdom and discipline matter.

Small groups, potentially the most versatile performance units of any organization, will increasingly make the difference in high-performance institutions. The reason is obvious: Leaders at all levels in most well-managed enterprises have already mastered the single-leader unit discipline. They recognize that a disciplined unit will outperform an effective group. Moreover, the advent of group work technology greatly favors the single-leader approach. Hence, team performance remains one of the most significant untapped opportunities for achieving higher and higher levels of performance competition demands. Integrating real-team performance capability into a more balanced leadership approach is well worth the effort. *Virtual teaming* is a promising development in this context, but only if such groups make conscious choices and apply the team discipline, as well as the single-leader discipline. Otherwise, the natural bias to pursue single-leader efforts will accelerate and performance potential will suffer.

Hence, we wrote this sequel and companion to *The Wisdom of Teams* to help you accomplish four simple things:

1. Clearly differentiate between effective groups and true performance units and consciously decide if and when you need a true performance unit.

2. Recognize the value of each of the two disciplines that characterize performance units and learn what each does best and how you can identify when and where to apply them.

3. Frequently practice evaluating performance challenges and making choices between the two disciplines to master the capability of applying the team discipline in concert with the single-leader discipline.

4. Understand what impact group work technology has on the performance of small groups, and learn how to make groupware work to your benefit.

These four accomplishments are much easier to describe and understand than they are to achieve. For that reason, we have tried to provide a set of exercises and tools to help small groups practice applying the different disciplines. Maybe it's an exaggeration to say practice makes perfect, but it is true that practice builds discipline. This book began with an example of how the USMC uses discipline to build pride and team-performance capability to become what they believe is the world's finest amateur fighting force. By that, the USMC means that most of its efforts are devoted to practicing to be ready for the few real wars Marines will fight. They practice tactical maneuvers, battlefield scenarios, as well as different team and single-leader configurations. Practice, practice, practice, until the performance-unit disciplines are ingrained in every marine. As a result, when the horrors of battle are upon them, they apply the right discipline in the right place at the right time.

We would not expect most small groups to achieve Marine levels of disciplined performance. We do, however, believe that your ability to get team, as well as single-leader, performance where it counts will improve with practice. The practice exercises and tools in this book are neither the only nor necessarily the best ones; however, they can be effective. And they can help groups design their own exercises, using similar tools and techniques. We also recognize that many of you must operate in working environments that create obstacles to sustaining the right balance between the two disciplines. Nonetheless, we are convinced that the best, most effective and adaptive organizations are and always will be guided by leaders at all levels who insist upon a disciplined integration of individual, team, and single-leader performance. Hence, in the emerging world of small-group performance, wisdom is discipline and discipline is wisdom.

INDEX

Mindbook-Workbook Series

Make Success Measurable! A Mindbook-Workbook for Setting Goals and Taking Action, by Douglas K. Smith

The Discipline of Teams: A Mindbook-Workbook for Delivering Small Group Performance, by Jon R. Katzenbach and Douglas K. Smith

Books by Jon R. Katzenbach

Peak Performance: Aligning the Hearts and Minds of Your Employees

Real Change Leaders

Teams At The Top

The Work of Teams

Books by Douglas K. Smith

Taking Charge of Change

Fumbling the Future: How Xerox Invented Then Ignored Personal Computing

Sources of the African Past

Books by Jon R. Katzenbach and Douglas K. Smith

The Wisdom of Teams